Old Age
is a Terminal Illness

How I Learned to Age Gracefully and Conquer My Fear of Dying

Alma H. Bond, Ph.D.

Universal Publishers
Boca Raton, Florida
USA • 2006

Old Age is a Terminal Illness:
How I Learned to Age Gracefully and Conquer My Fear of Dying

Universal Publishers
Boca Raton, Florida • USA
2006

ISBN: 1-58112-904-1

www.universal-publishers.com

Table of Contents

Introduction

I have been asked why I kept a death journal and why I have written this book. In the last decade, five dear friends died. When Kendall Kane*, my closest friend for twenty years, committed suicide two years ago, I went into a deep depression. For the first time in my life I found myself experiencing a writer's block. Neither consultations with colleagues, talking with friends who were still alive, nor time itself seemed to speed along the healing process. I still felt wretched and was unable to write.

Whenever I experience a conflict I do not understand, I keep a dream journal. I have done this since I was twenty-one years old. Studying my dreams often has helped me discover what is percolating in my unconscious, the first step toward resolution of the problem. For those readers who are not familiar with dream interpretation, I

---

* Kendall Kane and many other names in this book have been changed to protect the living. In addition, certain identifying facts have been modified. Nevertheless, in every case, I believe I have kept to the spirit of the truth.

quote Freud, "An unexamined dream is like an unopened letter." He meant that every dream carries a message within it. Else why dream the dream or read the letter?

What are the encoded communications in dreams? They consist chiefly of forbidden thoughts and situations that bring about great anxiety when brought to consciousness. Human beings are taught as children there are many thoughts and emotions that are "not nice." For example, "nice" children don't get angry or have sexual feelings. Therefore we shove the offending material to the bottom of our minds where it doesn't have to frighten us. Thus we can continue to feel we are good people whom mommy and daddy will find loveable, and we don't have to deal with the overwhelming anxieties triggered by "sinful" sensations. Unfortunately, once the objectionable material is pushed into the unconscious, for all ostensible purposes it is locked away and cannot be corrected by experience and maturity. For example, as adults, there is no need to repress sexuality, but many neurotic people continue to do so and live impoverished lives. People think we cannot bear the pain of grief, but it is surprising how much we can live with once we accept that there is no alternative. There are a number of ways sealed off material can seep back into consciousness, but insight into dream life, like a carefully read letter, is perhaps the most revealing.

When my "death depression" wouldn't heal, I made an effort to examine my dreams to determine the cause of the problem. This book is the tale of an odyssey to accept the inevitable, the deaths of those dear to me and the idea of my own demise.

My dream work made conscious that I was denying the entire aging process. Since I never gave it much thought, I wasn't in touch with my terror of dying. It was something that happened to other people, not me. While I would have denied it vociferously had anyone asked me, inside I felt impervious to death. But with people of my age dying like flies, it became impossible to keep away the knowledge that soon, too soon, the bell would toll for me.

You might ask why an analyst in practice for over thirty-five years would not be aware of such fears, without all the rigmarole of journals, dreams, etc. I was well aware of the ways in which I kept myself from knowing what I didn't want to know. Refusal to accept the idea of death is not the first time I experienced the need for such a defense, nor in all probability will it be the last. Denial is a mechanism I have used at each new phase of life. Until it was worked through, I denied my burgeoning sexuality as an adolescent, the passing of an era at menopause, and my grief at the deaths of my husband, mother, father, and brother. In similar manner, acceptance of my own seniority was hard to come by. Yet self-understanding is not something that is achieved once and for all, but is a hectic battle that must be re-fought by each of us at every stage of development. Each new phase of life necessitates a further undoing of defenses.

There is a lot of emotional work to be done before we can accept the inevitability of death. Isn't the real despair of the human condition that, street people or kings alike, eventually we all go the way of the cockroach? And there is nothing anyone or anything can do about it. Not doctors. Not diet. Not exercise. Not potions. Not lotions. Not creams. We die when we die. And I damn well better accept it.

This insight came to me in a dream about Rudy, my late husband Rudy, who died in 1982.

He is leaving the house and mumbling something about terminal illness. I am a bit incredulous, and sputter, "What...what?" I say perhaps there is some treatment for the condition. Rudy abruptly states, "Horse piss."

The doctor has prescribed an amber-colored pseudo-scientific concoction for me, ostensibly to prolong youth. It looks like Aslavital, the supposed cure for aging developed by Ana Aslan in Rumania, which I tried for a while. The liquid runs out of the faucet into the kitchen sink. I realize the "treatment" will be as useful to me as water is to cancer. I am going to die; if not now, soon enough. There are no two ways about it.

Rudy's comment, "horse piss," epitomizes his direct manner, his emotional honesty, and his awareness that there is nothing one can do to escape the painful exigencies of life.

How *does* one accept the idea that death is not far down the pike, when one is still healthy, vigorous, and in love with life? Freud believed that in the unconscious every one of us is convinced we will live forever. Such emotional blinders ward off feelings too painful to bear, and permit us to enjoy life. Nevertheless, there is a terrible emotional and physical cost for maintaining such illusions, and the truest wisdom lies in facing the seemingly intolerable. "If you want to endure life," Freud stresses, "prepare yourself for death."

My agent speaks of the WHIFM Factor, "What's in it for me?" What is in it for you, dear reader, should this book help you face the inevitability of your own death? Why would you want to pierce the iron veil of repression, which saves you so much pain and grief? Well, better health, for one thing, along with less conflict in daily living, and the likelihood of a fuller, richer life. Freud's greatest discovery is that fear of knowledge itself is the major cause of much illness. To constantly hold down the lid on fear is exhausting, and such depletion of energy keeps our capacities from unfolding to the fullest. Beneath the surface of repression lies the promise of improved emotional and physical health, as well as the possibility of developing all our potentialities.

When you accept that you are going to die, reader, each day becomes a gift. You are free to treasure each moment of love, memorize your children's faces, gently touch your grandchildren, glory in the sunset, and use your creativity to shape the golden years into the apex of your life.

Part 1: Alma Bond's Unexamined Musings

This chapter is largely the "intellectual part of the book." You are welcome to skip it, if you'd rather go on to the stories, but it is part of how I choose to think about death. My aim is to dissect it philosophically as well as emotionally and to examine what others wiser than I have said about it over the years.

May 14

I was swimming in a hotel pool. It was a cloudy, dreary day. My goggles had fallen into the water and slowly disappeared. I had jumped in after them, even though I was wearing a jacket. Electric wires were attached to the glasses, and I was afraid I would get a shock if I wore them.

When I awakened, I recalled a myth retold by Oliver Sacks in "The Island of the Colorblind[1]." Long ago on the island of Pohnpei in Micronesia there was a magic pool where the ruling Sandeleurs could see what was taking place on Pohnpei. After the brave hero Isohkelekel finally vanquished the Sandeleurs, he came to the pool. Looking down into its sacred waters, he saw the reflection of his aged face for the first time. He was so distraught he threw himself into the pool and drowned himself.

If so imposing a conqueror can be brought to suicide by viewing the ravages of age, what, I asked, can I expect of myself? I decided that if I really wanted to discover how I feel about "The undiscovered country, from whose bourne/ No traveler returns[2]," I'd better keep a "death journal" of my thoughts and feelings. A few nights later another dream confirmed my decision to keep this death journal.

May 17
There were lines in red on my computer where it asks for input, but the rest of the screen was in the shadows.

Growing old is a new role for me, and there is much about it I do not understand. The questions are written in my mind in blood red, but a black shadow shrouds the answers. I hope writing this journal will cast some light on the unknown and bring me to terms with my fear of dying. But then it's not dying itself that bothers me. I can live with that. The truth is I don't want to be dead! I feel like Woody Allen: "I'm not afraid to die. I just don't want to be there when it happens."

I was there when it almost happened. Ten years ago I was hit by a taxi, and knocked unconscious. I came close to dying, even to going through a "near-death experience" in which I was drawn to a light at the end of a tunnel. I woke up from a coma in the hospital with a concussion and seven broken bones. I discovered that dying isn't so bad: You simply don't wake up. Modern science confirms this by suggesting that we are equipped with a mechanism to make death easier, that when we are close to death we turn off suffering by releasing natural opiates called endorphins that block the experience of pain[3]. So I am not afraid to die; it is *not living* I find offensive.

Throughout the ages humankind has sought *ars moriendi*. Everybody seems to worry about achieving the "good death." I don't understand it. Of course it is desirable to avoid pain. Certainly if one has to die it would be good to die "well," preferably at home, surrounded by loved ones, with an absence of pain. Yes, that would be nice, if one <u>has</u> to die. But I don't understand the emphasis that people put on the kind of death they and those they love will experience. Even a bad death is no worse than the innumerable bouts of pain and loss we experience in a lifetime. These episodes passed. So will the instant of death. To me that's not what is most important. What matters is the life one has lived, if it was full, if it was gratifying, if one did and accomplished and loved as one wanted. *Dying is only one moment in time.* What matters to me is that it will be the end, and I will no longer be alive.

When one is in good health and in love with life, how *does* one comprehend the thought of leaving this earth? Sophocles[4] said it all twenty-four centuries ago when he wrote that the one thing in the universe that has defeated man is death:

"And he masters by his arts the beast whose lair is in the wilds...he tames the tireless mountain bull...and speech and windswept thought, and all the moods that mould a state, hath he taught himself; and how to flee the arrows of the frost...and the arrows of the rushing rain; yea, he hath resource for all; Without resource he meets nothing that must come: only against Death shall he call for aid in vain."

According to Freud[5], we all tend to "shelve" death, to eliminate it from our thinking, because the idea of an end to our consciousness is intolerable. In the unconscious, he says, every one of us is convinced of his own immortality. He gives an amusing example of the "normal attitude" to death, in which a man says to his wife, "If one of us dies, I shall go and live in Paris." I first became aware of this outlook as a child. Whenever anyone mentioned the possibility of dying, my mother, in a perfect demonstration of Freud's "normal attitude," would exclaim, "Bite your tongue!"

Freud said we have to live as if we were immortal, because otherwise for the average person the stress would be unbearable. Nevertheless, he advised if we would tolerate life, we should be prepared for death, because if the highest stake in living, life itself, is not at risk, life is impoverished and loses its interest.

Maybe. I'm not so sure. I don't think Freud was either. Elsewhere he wrote[6], "A flower that blossoms only for a single night does not seem to us on that account less lovely." I don't think visitors to Key West enjoy the perennial sunshine any more than its year round inhabitants do. The bougainvillea that blossoms eternally is just as lovely in my eyes as the roses that bloom in the springtime. Life is good enough as it is. I don't believe we need the idea of death to make us appreciate living.

To face the truth of death can be devastating and terrifying. The world is choked with violence and senseless accidents. We are destroying our beautiful planet. Soon we must die. What can possibly be offered in exchange for living with such anguish?

When I asked a friend who had recovered from a stroke and near death how he felt about his ordeal he said, "I feel a new sense of freedom. When you've faced the worst, you've done it already. There's nothing to be afraid of anymore. You think, oh, here's another day; you'd better not waste it. I'll never be unhappy about trivialities again."

I'm told that if I can accept the idea of my own death, my life too will become more precious. Each day will be a gift. I will memorize my children's faces, lovingly stroke my grandchildren, tell my friends I love them, and eagerly write what might be my last book. But then I do these things anyway. It seems less and less like a bargain.

There must be something good about dying; Kingsley Amis[7] found something he liked about it:

Death has got something to be said for it:
There's no need to get out of bed for it;
Wherever you may be,
They bring it to you, free.

But I'll cast my lot with Shakespeare[8], who said, "Of comfort no man speak. / Let's talk of graves, of worms, and epitaphs."

May 19
(The night after I began this journal)
I dreamed of a headless man staggering around like a chicken without a head.

When I awoke, I recalled the time my mother had taken me to a kosher butcher shop. Standing in a room stinking of bloody chicken coops piled on a sawdust floor, I watched the proprietor yank a squawking chicken by the neck and slam it against a wooden block. Then, hoisting a bloody ax, she whacked it down on the screaming chicken's head. Imagine my disbelief when the decapitated chicken lunged up from the block and wobbled down the length of the entire counter, its neck gushing blood straight up in the air like a geyser.

"Verte geharget, gey in drerd!" (Drop dead, go to Hell) shouted the woman, as she chased the chicken down the room.

No, no, my experiences with death are not designed to make it appealing. I'm with Jesus, when he said, "Let the dead bury their dead[9]."

John Wheeler, in Lisl Goodman's[10] *Death and the Creative Life*, says that a great spreading tree kills the future for promising young trees that are too close to it. "Death is essential for renewal," he said. "The world is renewed from underneath."

My father was "a great spreading tree" with the desire to preserve the future for his children. He had advanced diverticulosis, and was close to death. I've never felt he had to die. I believe if he had tried harder, he could have made it. But he told me he didn't want to use up all his money on heroic efforts to save his life. His death was a sacrifice that enabled him to leave an inheritance to his children. He died for us.

Like my father, I don't want to kill the future for "promising young trees." But science is learning to keep us alive long past the given biblical life span. Why not root for technology finding room for us all, such as expanding civilization to other planets or developing life beneath the sea? Trash is recycled; why not recycle the old and the dying into new roles of mentors and role models? Young people could benefit from their wisdom and experience.

Perhaps science will advance in its fight against the decay of human powers to the point where a human life will be terminated only by unforeseeable accident. In that distant utopia, the time between human birth and death will expand beyond any limits imaginable today, and like a well tended old car, what psychoanalyst Alex H. Kaplan[11] called "the rusting years" will be kept at bay all our lives. Then the kind of thinking I saw on a bumper sticker: "The older I get the better I used to be," will no longer be appropriate.

May 20

No! I'm definitely not in a hurry to leave this incredibly beautiful world. I intend to snub the uninvited guest as long as I can, and try to behave as the great activist and philanthropist Lily Peter planned[12]:

Tell Death I am not here,
When he comes for me.
He will find me standing yonder
Under a quince tree,
With violets in my hair
Jasmine in my hand,
Looking for the last time
At the lovely land:

Feeling for the last time
The wind in my face
Watching the clouds go over
In their tall grace,

Death may have the body
In the room at the head of the stair,
But I shall be under a quince tree
With violets in my hair.

I find it touching that Lily Peter's friends saw to it that she was buried under a quince tree with violets in her hair. But I say, spare me the quince tree, with or without violets. No, I won't make it easy for Death to claim me. I will kick and scream and holler and make such a racket it will chase him away, more like Edna St. Vincent Millay[13] than Lily Peters:

Withstanding Death
Till Life be gone,
I shall treasure my breath,
I shall linger on.

I shall bolt my door

With a bolt and a cable;
I shall block my door
With a bureau and a table;

With all my might
My door shall be barred.
I shall put up a fight,
I shall take it hard.
With his fist on my mouth
He shall drag me forth,
Shrieking to the south
And clutching at the north.

May 21

I read a lot about death these days. Anatole Broyard[14] impresses me with his notion that the patient must treat his disease not as a disaster or an occasion for depression and panic, but as a narrative or story. In that way, Broyard says, the writer has an antibody against illness and pain.

What a good idea, I think. So I pull out my neglected notebook from under the pile of *Victoria's Secret* silk underpants and determine to write the "narrative" of my journey to the grave.

Eliot Jacques[15] says that one of the crucial aspects of emotional maturity is to resign oneself to the aging process, to assimilate one's true age, to stop pretending that life has no end. He says there is a need for "self-mourning" or grieving for the inevitability of one's own eventual death.

I guess that's what I've been doing lately, mourning the inevitability of my own death, along with the deaths of my friends. When I saw the Key West turquoise sea the other day, my eyes teared up as I realized I may not be standing there admiring it many more times. Seeing my grandchildren last weekend made me cry as I pictured how sad they would be at my funeral, as distressed as my seven-year-old son Zane was at the funeral of my mother. When he cried, it made me cry even more.

Yes, Broyard has something. Writing about aging can be an antibody against depression.

15

Broyard believed that one must be ill and die with style[16]. He found a way of being an invalid that was unique to him, and died with elegance and grace. Ill people can go on being themselves. Perhaps even more so than before, for each person has a distinctive way of being ill. In the depth of his infirmity, all Broyard's old, trivial selves dissolved and he was reduced to his essence.

Fritjof Capra[17] quotes Carlos Castenada in a similar philosophy, to the effect that "An immense amount of pettiness is dropped if your death makes a gesture to you, or if you catch a glimpse of it...Death is the only wise adviser that we have."

I had seen such a transformation in my son Zane after he recovered from a debilitating illness. He waited in line at a restaurant for an hour to be seated for his dinner.

"Weren't you angry?" I asked him.

"No," he said. "I've learned the hard way what is important."

Let's hope I can do the same. Right now my style of aging seems to be grumbling and bemoaning the passage of time. Perhaps I can find my own style of growing old, so that when the time comes, I too can leave the earth in a manner unique to myself.

During his illness Broyard utilized every sensation to expand his consciousness while waiting "for the next phase[18]." He believed "Illness is primarily a drama, and it should be possible to enjoy it as well as to suffer it." I'm not so sure. My philosophy is more like that of psychologist Erving Goffman's, who speaks of the "spoiled identity of the sick[19]." When I read such lines as, "O death, where is thy sting? O Grave, where is thy victory?[20]" I can only mutter, "Whistling in the dark...."

May 24

The final pages of the life of the artist Wilem de Kooning, as told by Calvin Tompkins[21], tell a different kind of tale about life winning out over death. It is similar to Broyard's in that both men preserved their "style" until their late years. When De Kooning was ninety-three years old, he was virtually immobilized by Alzheimer's Disease. In 1978,

16

after a lifetime of drinking, the artist was an alcoholic disaster. With the support of his ex-wife, Elaine de Kooning, he began a program of psychotherapy and Alcoholics Anonymous, during which he "recovered" from alcoholism. During this period, he painted little, but came out of it with a new style of painting. He formerly had been a perfectionist in his art, sometimes painting the same work hundreds of times. Perhaps in his therapy (as frequently happens) his conscience softened up.

According to Tom Ferrara, one of his two major assistants, de Kooning "made a conscious decision to be less self-critical." Tompkins says, "The paintings became less and less crowded, the fluid, undulating forms more clearly defined." During this period, the artist worked frantically, turning out a painting a week. He would begin by sketching a few abstract forms, usually borrowed from one of his earlier works, and then would paint in and around them, reworking as he proceeded. According to Tompkins, "the late paintings have an airy lightness and a lyricism for which there is no precedent in a half century of the artist's work."

Many artists paint in different styles at different periods of their lives. What is uncanny about de Kooning is that although practically incapacitated by Alzheimer's, he nevertheless continued to paint until the age of ninety. How could it be that someone incapable of signing his name, who was unable to function in the most basic aspects of living, was able to paint in a manner some compare to the late style of Matisse's cut-paper masterpieces? Tompkins quotes the neurologist Oliver Sacks, who says he has seen "all sorts of skills (including artistic ones) preserved or largely preserved, even in advanced stages of dementing diseases such as Alzheimer's...Style, neurologically, is the deepest part of one's being, and may be preserved, almost to the last, in a dementia."

I have always felt that creativity and the source of life are of a piece, and that when we are able to understand one, we will also understand the other. The other day, my granddaughters and I were working on a few pieces of sculpture. When we finished, there stood a little man and his dog, looking as alive as we did. It was uncanny. Out of

17

nothing, a lump of clay, there now was something. It reminded me of the feeling I had on first seeing Zane as a newborn child. There was nothing there, and then all of a sudden, there was a person!

Out of nothing, the gases in the universe became the planets and the stars. Out of nothing comes something. That is the similarity between life and creativity. In one's creative self reposes the essence of being, a mini-example of the origin of life. No wonder creative people tend to live a long time. De Kooning was on to this similarity. In one of his last interviews, he said, "You have to keep on the very edge of something, all the time, or the picture dies." The person dies too, Mr. de Kooning.

May 30

Why am I even thinking about death? Even the bible says, "A living dog is better than a dead lion[22]." Like Edna St. Vincent Millay[23], I am interested only in living:

Life must go on,

And the dead forgotten;

Life must go on,

Though good men die;

Ann, eat your breakfast;

Dan, take your medicine;

Life must go on;

I forget just why.

My seven-year-old granddaughter Mia apparently is also worried about my approaching demise. Reading a questionnaire which asked the respondent to check the proper age box, Mia said sadly, "You're in the last box of life, Nana."

Jungian psychoanalyst Lisl Goodman[24] suggests a technique for living comfortably and intimately with death that interests me. She makes a number of daring recommendations, including that we reckon our age by counting not from birth onward but from death backward, based on how much longer we can reasonably expect to live. Oh goody, I quipped to the mourning dove keening in my garden. Since I'm planning to live to be one hundred, this means I am only thirty years old.

I often think about Philip Kane, the handsome, forty-year-old blond and blue-eyed son of Kendall, who was the most recent of my intimate friends to die. Although Philip was terminally ill with cancer, he refused to give up. He hadn't slept or eaten for weeks, or expelled waste products. His massive stomach bulged through the bedclothes. Finally, Philip decided to give in to the inevitable. He kissed his wife and children goodbye and lay back in his bed to die. He lay there a long moment. Nothing happened. He tried some more. Still nothing happened. A peculiar expression dented his bloated face.

"What's wrong, dearest?" his wife asked.

"I never died before," Philip replied. "I don't know how to do it."

Bertram, my friend Anna's husband, feels equally rejecting of death. His pal of a lifetime died recently. Thinking, no doubt, of his flourishing chiropractic practice, his wife, children and grandchildren, Bert declared, "Not me! I'm not going to die and give up all this!"

Arnold Hutchnecker, Richard Nixon's psychoanalyst, said, "The strong and mighty fear death most[25]."

These men must be among the strong of the earth, I mused this morning as I brushed my teeth and squinted in the mirror at my curly (dyed) dark brown hair cut around my only slightly crinkled face, and well-exercised figure which has not changed much except to improve for thirty years. (I started exercising at age forty.) I've spent more than half a century becoming my own person, developing the talents I was born with, trying to overcome my shortcomings, broadening and curtailing my appetites, learning to live with disappointment and sorrow, standing with some dignity in the closed world of men, and transcending the animal condition.

I am no longer driven by uncontrollable urges or stamped out of any mold. I have learned to be a good enough daughter, wife, friend, lover, mother, scholar, and writer. It has taken me seventy years to fashion all this, and now it seems I am fit only as a target for the Grim Reaper. Isn't this the real despair of the human condition, that whatever our value to humankind we must go the way of the ant and the fruit fly? Moliere said it: "Life is a play with a badly written third act."

Psychoanalyst Sam Atkin[26] had a philosophy similar to Broyard's, which kept him joyous and life-seeking to the moment of death at the end of his ninetieth year. Despite being severely ill with Parkinson's disease and often unable to speak or sit upright, he considered his life "a journey into the creation of the ever new phases of existence." Incredibly, he was able to continue with his practice and writing his papers, and through his own capacity to overcome defeat and despair, teach his patients to do the same.

I greatly admire these creative men, but fear I cannot emulate their heroic stance. I am too angry at the idea of falling off the horse at what feels to me like midstream. Everyone tells me I am the picture of health, and look at least fifteen years younger than my age. Recently I went to my Scandinavian physician with various minor complaints. The youthful doctor didn't take them seriously. "You are a lucky woman," he said. "In Sweden nobody your age runs two miles a day or has all their teeth."

"Remind me never to visit Sweden!" I replied.

June 6

A prescient dream warned me I had better prepare myself for what lay ahead.

The dream pictured a cat, with beautiful multi-striped fur of orange and brown, who playfully leaped onto my lap. A voice announced that the creature will need blood transfusions one day, and should prepare for that eventuality by putting aside blood now.

Much as I fight the knowledge, a spasm in my intestines insists that the message in the dream is authentic, and I should begin to build all possible assets, physical, financial, social, and emotional, as a bulwark against the problems old age almost certainly will bring.

Little things are beginning to go awry. My balance is not what it used to be. (I bought a book about improving balance in old age, but I keep forgetting to read it.) My teeth are beginning to chip and crack-last year I needed two new caps. I who was once known for my "iron" stomach have joined that battalion of people I formerly considered pitiful who can't eat fats and can't eat sweets and can't eat this and that because it is "hard to digest." In discussing his digestive problems, my friend Sol Dorman said that people who ride a bicycle don't produce as much gas. Standing in line in a packed theatre lobby, Sol called out, "Somebody in here hasn't been riding a bicycle." I hope I won't have to do a lot more bicycle riding.

My "perfect" heart has begun to palpitate a bit now and then. I say, "Stop that, heart! I won't have it!" Sometimes it actually does. But it has never needed instruction before.

My back goes out more than it used to, and I have recently become a regular visitor to the chiropractor. The calcium level in my bones is slowly dropping, and medication has been prescribed to prevent osteoporosis. My cholesterol is too high, and I have begun treatment or that, too. My list of medications is expanding geometrically every year. But as the expression goes, it's better than the alternative. I feel like the Mexican American described by Studs Terkel[27], whose buddy was sad that his friend needed to walk with a cane. The lame man replied, "It beats not walking at all." True. Nevertheless, Mr. Shakespeare had it right when he said, "From hour to hour we ripe and ripe, from hour to hour we rot and rot, and thereby hangs a tale[28]."

June 8

When I was five years old I saw a movie called *Just Imagine*. It pictured a future in which people swallowed pills dispensed by a slot machine, instead of eating food. What with calcium, amino acids, vitamin A, B's, C, D, zinc, selenium, pantothenic acid, PABA, and beta-carotene, *Just Imagine* is no longer a fantasy: the future is now.

Fighting old age means waging a war on many fronts. There is the physical aspect, fought primarily by diet. What is important is not just what you eat, but what you don't eat: Gone forever are the noble treats of yesteryear, like ice cream, cake, and candy. In its place we are permitted soups, salads, and delicious treats like cauliflower and broccoli. To my mind, the best thing the first President Bush ever said was, "I am President of the United States, and if I don't want to eat broccoli, I don't have to!" In one prison, where inmates in solitary confinement need further discipline, their diet is changed. All sugar, salt, fats, and meats are removed from their menu. When I read that, I thought, just like my Pritikin diet! (I'm only kidding-it really isn't so bad.)

Of course we must exercise daily. Swimming, running, or riding my exercycle for at least a half hour has become as automatic as brushing my teeth. But it is not enough just to exercise. My daughter, the nutritionist, says I cannot merely swim; I must also run and lift weights for the ultimate good of my bone density. When my doctor at Pritikin watched me swimming, he said, "You swim like a mermaid, but you must go faster to raise your heart rate." When I told my friend Arlene Richards what the doctor had said, she commented, "You won't live longer; it will just seem that way!"

We must have a physical examination every six months, with annual flu shots a necessity after sixty-five, not to mention the gynecologist, the eye, ear and nose specialist, the audiologist, and the ophthalmologist we oldsters are supporting so nicely.

For each part of the body there must be a guardian: Mevacor to keep down cholesterol, aspirin to guard against strokes and heart disease, calcium supplements and Fosamax to avoid osteoporosis, and now it is even suggested that Ibuprofen can help stave off Alzheimer's Disease.

Then there is one's emotional health, which is developed through lifelong study of the self, if we are fortunate enough to be able to skip the therapists and counselors. If one knows oneself, it is easier to follow the rest of the health regime. And let us not forget the spiritual self, for those so inclined. And the philosophical aspect: what cannot be changed must be accepted. And there are the unexpected guerilla fighters that can fire pot shots at any time: to avoid them one must go through the yearly terrors of mammograms and pap tests. And of course the usual biannual trip to the dentist, the more numerous teeth cleanings necessitated by the natural yellowing of teeth that have been around for almost three quarters of a century, and the ever more frequent flossing demanded by the aging process. And the chiropractor for the back, of course, along with the daily exercises for back strengthening.

Then there are the little irritants like eye drops and anti-histamines for allergies, the requisite protein base for one's nails, less they split and crack, and the fact that one's calluses must be trimmed and foot fungus fought. We need Retin-A to avoid wrinkles (hah!), skin moisturizer for the face, hair moisturizer for the hair, lotion for the body, a different sort for the hands, etc., etc., etc. And we won't even begin to discuss what is necessary to sustain the health and regularity of the digestive system. No wonder people retire. We haven't time to do anything but take care of our health. And that's for a well person! I understand what my friend's husband meant when he said his wife looked as good as ever; it is just that maintenance takes longer. I didn't realize how much time and money I spend on preservation of my health and appearance until I began to catalog this list.

I had my hearing checked recently, and the otolaryngologist said it was fine.

"But it is not as good as it used to be," I protested.

"It's not supposed to be," he laughed.

One night while I was reading Ernest Becker's *Denial of Death*[29], the lights seemed dim.

"Uh oh," I said aloud, "It's happening! I knew it. My vision is beginning to go!"

Then the lights flickered and went back on full force. It was only a power outage. But I wasn't too relieved. It'll happen sooner or later.

If anything is going to go wrong, I want advance notice. When I was forty-seven years old, I couldn't find the eye of the needle. I, who always had twenty\twenty vision, panicked. I'll bet I have Glaucoma, I thought. I went immediately to an ophthalmologist, who examined my eyes and said I was merely suffering from presbyopia, or old age vision.

"Didn't anyone tell you that people in their forties become far-sighted?" he asked.

No, nobody had. I want to make good and sure that kind of surprise doesn't slip up on me again. I feel like a friend who developed a severe case of arthritis and chastised her mother: "Why didn't you tell me getting old was like this?" But then I probably wouldn't have listened if anyone *had* told me. I remember my father saying, "It's tough to get old!" Now, when it is too late, I regret not having asked him what he meant.

I now need an eye check-up twice a year. "Your vision is excellent," the ophthalmologist reassured me, "I just want to keep checking for cataracts and macular degeneration."

I sprinted to my *Merck's Manual*[30], where the disease is listed as Macular Degeneration of the Aged. The physician told me he was not worried about it. Nevertheless he gave me an Amsler Grid to reveal pigmentary or hemorrhagic disturbance in the macular region of my left eye.

According to Merck (p. 3223), "No medical therapy is effective." But all is not lost. It advises, "Patients should be informed they will not lose all sight."

Thank God for small favors! But such deterioration is a harbinger of worse to come, to say nothing of the final departure blueprinted for us all. How I hate that little speech the flight attendants give just before the plane lands, when they lecture on disembarking at your final destination! I don't know about my fellow passengers, but I have no intention of making the landing my final destination on earth.

I am convinced that airlines are insensitive to the feelings of their aging population. Evidence can be found in the receipt handed out by a well-known airline when I purchased a ticket recently to visit my daughter Janet. The voucher listed times and airports for the journey, etc. etc. Then, at the bottom of the slip, I was shocked to see a huge END.

Are the airlines trying to get rid of their Senior Citizens? Why not write "End of trip," or "Hope to see you again?"

Another expression I hate is killing time. Why would anyone want to, when it is so precious? There are so many things to do. When I have a few minutes before a guest arrives, I listen to the news or read the second string mail I've put aside or do those little jobs like paying bills that I detest. I might even, God forbid, straighten up the house. I refuse to kill time. It is all we have.

And then there is "time is money". What an insult to humanity that one is! Time is life. Time is joy. Time is beauty. The one thing it is not is money.

This morning my bedroom was an ungodly mess. (The more I write, the less I clean.) Better tidy up, I told myself. It would be dreadful if you dropped dead, and people found you keeled over in the middle of this pigsty!

I know why I am so touchy about intimations of mortality. Everybody says "You look good for your age." But slowly, slowly, I am realizing that I have begun the downward slide that is the lot of all living species. I am beginning to glimpse my final destination, the END.

June 18

In contrast to adolescence, where the sensation is like living in a house being constructed around one, old age feels as if one is occupying a home that is crumbling. Loss of height, weight gain, wrinkles, and a matronly spread of hip and thigh have altered the appearance of many of my friends. Some of them are unable to accept the fact that they have changed and thus are unable to correct their self image. As Faith Baldwin said, "Time is a dressmaker specializing in alterations." And the alterations rarely make for a better fit. Unlike my death-denying friends who remain in a fool's paradise each alteration leaves me breathless, as though I had been punched in the stomach.

Life is a world class boxer; no sooner have I recovered from one blow than it socks me another. Nevertheless, I prefer acknowledging painful facts rather than deceiving myself. At least that is what I tell myself. But looking at the naked truth is not always easy to do. I pity an acquaintance who was once a beautiful actress, but fails to realize she now is old, with sagging body and wrinkled face. This woman continues to flirt with men young enough to be her sons, who laugh behind her back and make dates with her and fail to show up.

The fine actor, Gene Hackman, also experiences difficulty in accepting the inevitable changes of aging. "I read a story and say, 'That would be great for me.' Then I realize it would've been great for me forty years ago!"

A friend of a certain age laughingly told me she was standing in line at *Victoria's Secret* to pay for a sexy nightgown she hoped would restore her husband's languishing sexual proficiency. Behind her stood a woman of perhaps twenty years of age buying the same nightgown. My friend was delighted, and congratulated herself on her youthful selection. She said, "I see we have the same taste in nightgowns."

"Oh, yes," the young woman said. "I am buying it for my grandmother."

I glow proudly when I note that my body transformations are still somewhat minor, a one inch loss in height, a few wrinkles, and the graying of my hair, remedied monthly at Hot Cuts Beauty Salon. At a party the other evening, a woman who appeared to be in her late seventies told me she had a daughter around my age.

"How old is your daughter?" I asked.

"She is 51."

I laughed, thanked her, and told her I was a lot closer to her age than her daughter's.

Nevertheless, the discrepancy between my self-image and appearance became pitifully apparent a few weeks ago when I passed a group of men on the sidewalk. As a young woman I pretended to ignore such gatherings to discourage them from whistling or making suggestive remarks. On this day, I walked by the group and took my usual pains to look in the opposite direction. But my stomach dropped to my boot tops when I realized that no one was looking at me.

A cartoon in *The New Yorker*[31] says it all. A woman tells a man of similar age, "You're really nice, Richard. I was hoping I could fix you up with my mom." Something like that actually happened to me. My young doctor asked me if I would like to go out with his grandfather. I thought, "I'd rather go out with you!"

I like to believe that shocks such as these woke me up

to reality, but, alas, I am hit over and over again with the truth. I see a woman on the bus, and think, what a lovely (homely, kind, mean, deformed, etc.) old lady! Then I'm startled to realize that the old lady is younger than I. I recently looked at a picture of my grandmother, an elderly woman with silver hair twisted into a bun, and suddenly realized that the Grandmother in the photo is twenty years younger than I am now. Imagine being twenty years older than your own grandmother! Impossible. Somebody is making it all up. Or God is playing a terrible joke on us.

I am beginning to understand that the process of surrendering to my new stage of life will last a long time before it is over. And then further changes will certainly occur. I'm just getting used to being middle aged, and now I have to adjust to growing old!

June 21

And oh, the sensitivities of aging! Surely I have never been so tearful before. Well, maybe when I was a teenager. Yesterday I treated myself to lunch alone at Shoney's, where I sometimes enjoy the soup and salad bar. After finishing the excellent pizza soup, I left my *Writer's Digest* and ice tea at my booth, and went to the bar to claim my salad. When I returned, I found my table wiped clean, and the magazine and tea gone. I checked carefully around the restaurant, thinking perhaps I had been mistaken about my table. When it became apparent that my memory was correct, I turned to the waiter with a perplexed expression. He hurriedly brought more tea and with burning face retrieved the sodden magazine from the garbage can. To my embarrassment, I burst into tears! It helped a little that I wasn't charged for my lunch.

Reading about the musical, *Steel Pier* (where I had spent many hours as a child) made me cry. I even cry at the idea of crying. The thought of music in the Miserere scene in *Il Trovatore* in which Leonore is dying, makes me cry. When she sings that love shall conquer death, I think, oh sure! But I cry anyway.

On the other hand, something in me is not surprised at my down hill trail. When I was five years old, in the days

27

when little chicks were sold for pets at Easter time in five and dime stores like Woolworth's, I was thrilled when my parents brought home a chick. I called it Sweetie-Tweetie, and it became the joy of my lonely life. The first thing every morning I darted down the two flights of stairs to greet Sweetie-Tweetie. Then I carefully fed and played with it until it was time to leave for kindergarten.

But my family also had a cat. One day, when I came downstairs to greet my pet, I was horrified to see that the chick only had one eye. Nobody understood what had happened until a feather was observed on one of the cat's paws. The next morning, I dashed downstairs again, only to find that the chick now had no eyes left. And on the third day, there was no chick at all.

The lesson bored through my brain like my father's electric drill. This is the way life is, I sobbed. You start out with everything, and then bit by bit, you lose it all. Later, when a pair of my favorite paisley curtains began to droop, I told myself, of course. You learned that would happen when you were five years old.

June 22

As I was driving home from a lunch date, stopping my car for a red light, I noticed a frail old woman shuffling her feet along the sidewalk. She had thin white hair with bald spots showing through, and walked at almost a forty-five degree angle. Her color was sickly beige, and her skin was pasty. I stared at her and wondered, is that how I'll look twenty years from now? The lesson resurfaced again.

When she saw me looking at her, she beckoned with a finger like the witch in Hansel and Gretel checking whether Hansel was fat enough to eat. I lowered my window.

"Would you drive me home?" she asked.

"Certainly," I answered, getting out and opening the door. The woman must need the ride badly, I thought, or she wouldn't ask. I may need that kind of help myself some day. If I do I hope someone will do the same for me. As the cars honked about us, the woman stood there doubled up as if in pain. I worried she wasn't going to make it to the car.

"Are you all right?" I asked.

28

"Yes, I'm fine," the woman answered, making an obvious effort to respond energetically.

The cars honked raucously, as I helped her totter into the car. How selfish can people get? I thought. Can't they see a person is in trouble here?

Then I worried that the woman might have a heart attack or a stroke in the car before I got her home. What would I do then? I'd have to take her to the hospital. I shouldn't have looked at her. Have I taken on more than I can handle?

It seemed she wasn't sure where she lived. "It's at the top of the hill," she cackled. I couldn't see any hill at all.

"It's off Southard, on Griffin Lane." I drove down Southard, which was one way, and back up Fleming, the next street. Still no Griffin Lane.

"It's where the old hospital used to be."

I had no idea where the old hospital used to be, and kept driving round and round the block. What have I gotten myself into?

I yanked out a map, was able to locate the lane, and drove by where I thought it should be. I hope she doesn't die in the car before I get her home, I thought. What would I do then? Take her to the police station, I guess.

"There, you passed it," the woman said, self-importance flaring up like a fever. "You passed it!"

Once more I drove around the block. I was getting wearier and wearier and thought, if I don't find it soon, I'm going to take her to the police station even if she's still alive!

"There, that's it," the old woman said, a bent finger pointing to an unmarked lane hidden in a cove off the side of the road. "I live in there. Drive me in."

Relieved, I drove into the narrow way, barely managing to get through the double row of overgrown bushes. Some branches grated against my car, and I hoped they weren't scratching it. I considered asking the woman to get out and walk the short distance that remained, but then thought, the hell with it. It's worth paying a mechanic a few dollars to get rid of the old crone!

I continued driving up the lane, which was more like a path, until we reached a small sagging house painted in a peeling pink. The house looked as if it were preparing for molting, as befitted its occupant's time of life.

"How much do I owe you?" the woman asked, making an effort to pull herself up straight.

"You don't owe me anything."

"No," she insisted. "I would have had to take a cab." She fumbled around in her limp purse, took out two dollars, and pressed them into my hands.

I struggled over whether to accept the money. I really didn't want to. She was obviously impoverished, and I was sorry for her. On the other hand, allowing her to pay for the ride might keep her from feeling like a charity case. I took the two dollars.

June 23

Last night I had another dream.

An ancient lady was leaning over a baby in her crib. On the woman's head was a huge bald spot, splotched with tiny red eruptions. The baby began to scream.

I wondered if the dream was a memory and called my older sister, Pauline. "Yes," she said. "That must have been Meme Sura, our great aunt. She had a disease called Alopecia, and lost part of her hair." Is it any wonder I have qualms about aging?

The dream brought another memory to mind. I was a young woman who had already started my lifelong practice of daily swimming. An elderly woman often doddered into the locker room when I was getting ready to swim. I watched with disbelief each day as the ancient swimmer dragged herself to the pool. This day, she came in leaning on a walker, and could barely stand up long enough to put on her bathing suit. "Why doesn't she give up already?" I said to a fellow swimmer. My friend coughed surreptitiously and made a few spastic movements with her elbow. I turned around to see what she was trying to tell me, and saw that the old woman was right behind me and probably had overheard what I said. My face burned as if I'd been skewered in a barbecue pit.

Whatever was wrong with me, that I had so little empathy for an aging person? Perhaps I didn't want to

30

know about my own fate. I feel different about the old swimmer now. I admire her pluck and determination to stay alive. I wish I could apologize to her but she must have died a long time ago. Although with that spunky lady, who knows! I vow to be ultra kind and thoughtful to people older than myself, if there are still any around.

My fantasy: She is in Heaven looking down at me, and with spastic movements of her elbow gestures to God to hurl a bolt of lightening that will knock me into my swimming pool.   She cackles, heh, heh, that's what you get for making that nasty crack.

Another memory that haunts me happened around the same time.   My mother was dying of a cerebral hemorrhage in the hospital. In the bed next to her was an old woman, or what once had been an old woman. She had also suffered a stroke, or perhaps a series of them, and was unable to move, see, or even to hear. The only part of her anatomy that seemed to function was her mouth. An attendant stood over the creature feeding her lunch. After each spoonful, she opened her shriveled mouth like a baby bird awaiting its next mouthful. The image of that wasted, withering body living only for the next spoonful flashes into my mind over and over, when I contemplate the potential dangers of aging. At moments like those, I think my mother was better off dying when she did, even at a relatively young age.

Agonizing about these old women and the preview of what lies in store for me, I watched a TV program that made me feel even worse: As if it isn't bad enough to lose a loved one, I learned the government is appointing a task force to investigate fraud in cemeteries. It seems relatives of the deceased have discovered a second casket of a stranger buried directly on top of their kin. In addition, old tomb stones have been broken and plowed under, and expensive caskets drilled with holes to allow water to run off. The relatives are forming a protest group.

My horror receded when another, kinder story about a graveyard surfaced: A couple traveling the United States in search of unknown heroes came across a man who had discovered the unmarked graves of children who died during the Depression, when their parents couldn't afford to buy gravestones. He has erected markers on their graves.

Graveyards remind me of funeral parlors and the day of our mother's funeral. The receptionist who met my sister Pauline and me at the chapel greeted us with a painted smile, as false as a wooden leg. Her expression was so brittle she looked as if her cheeks would crack if she extended them a fraction farther. It felt terrible to be inundated with grief, and feel forced to respond to a phony smile. Whatever was wrong with her? Did she think her good humor would raise our spirits and make us stop grieving? Was she stupid, or just trying to deny death along with the rest of us? Pauline charged into the business office and said we refused to work with that woman. She asked the funeral parlor to supply us with someone more empathic. It did.

I also hated the sermon the rabbi gave at the funeral. He spoke impersonally of a good Jewish woman, who loved her husband and children, and was beloved in the community. He could have been talking about any one of a vast population of women. There was not one word in the eulogy that specifically described Bertha Halbert. Apparently he was unacquainted with the expression, "God is in the details." What he said about her may well have been true, but how would he know? He had never met my mother.

A story about such a eulogy appeared recently in the *Readers Digest*[32]. The writer, Robin Greenspan, knows a pastor who also uses a standard liturgy for funerals. To make them more personal, he presses the find and replace key on his computer to locate the name of the deceased from the previous funeral and replace it with that of the newly departed. For one liturgy, the pastor requested his computer to find every instance the name "Mary" appeared and to replace it with "Edna."

At the next service, the congregation was surprised to read from the preprinted program, "Jesus Christ, born of the Virgin Edna."

In contrast to the eulogies of the "Virgin Edna" and my mother, a rabbi who cared to find out about Bertha Halbert might have said something like this:

She was a shy immigrant girl of eighteen when she

came over to the United States from a small town in Romania. She had gone only to the fourth grade, but frequently said, "Over there you learned more in elementary school than they teach here in high school." Nevertheless, she always felt inadequate among American women. 'Did Mrs. Holtz go to high school?' she would ask, about the mothers of her daughters' friends. Not knowing a word of English when she arrived, she fought valiantly to learn the language of a strange and frightening land. With no one to teach her, she battled her way through books like *War and Peace* and *The Brothers Karamazov* and learned to speak credible English.

In earlier times in a rustic setting, she might have been a more contented person, for she remained a simple woman in a complicated, confusing world. A genuine homemaker, she tried her best to be the kind of mother she thought her children needed, making sure they ate the best foods, drank their milk regularly, and were given the best health care she could provide. That she was only partially successful was due more to the mismatch between her and her culture than to a lack of caring.

She was a welcoming, giving hostess, and the extended family used her home as a gathering place. Many was the Sabbath meal on Friday evening that saw twenty people gathered around her lavishly stocked dinner table, overflowing with the chopped liver, babaganouch, roasted peppers, moma liga (farina with sauce), chicken noodle soup with delicious unborn eggs taken from the chicken, roast chicken with tastily prepared vegetables and her home baked chocolate cake. "Take more, there is plenty," was a typical remark to guests. She was a sweet, dedicated wife and her husband adored her, 'Your mother is your best friend,' he would frequently tell his offspring. Her main joy in life was her children, and her great sorrow was the child she lost a short while ago.

She was a brave woman, who tried to keep her enduring grief from her family. She spent many a day crying on her bed, after her family left home. I believe her grief at her son's death broke her heart and caused her death, too.

June 28

I've been inundated with deaths lately, three more in the past two months. When my first old uncle died years ago, I was deeply depressed for months. I remember thinking, only half facetiously, that it might be less painful if my other five uncles and their wives would all die at the same time. Picturing them buried together in a giant pit like the Nazis dug for their victims, I thought I could mourn all ten together and keep my life from being swamped in grief for years. Funny, there is something to the old saying to be careful what you wish for because you may get it. Now I really have a deluge of deaths to grieve about at the same time. But maybe I was right in the first place: Perhaps I can mourn all my friends together and get it over with.

I search everywhere for words of wisdom about death, but rarely meet with success. When it comes to the great art of dying, we are all novices like Philip Kane. In Montiverdi's opera, *The Coronation of Poppea*, I eagerly looked forward to the death scene of the philosopher Seneca, anticipating that at last I would hear some great thinking on the subject. But I'm afraid Seneca was not much wiser than the rest of us, when it comes to leaving this vale of tears.

(To messenger who brings the news that Emperor Nero, Seneca's former pupil, has ordered him to kill himself for conspiring to have Poppea murdered) Seneca: "If you bring me death you need not ask for forgiveness. I laugh when you bring me such a fine present. Friend, the hour has come when I am to practice the virtue I praise. Death is a brief agony, a wandering sigh that leaves the heart where for many years it has stayed as a guest. Like a wanderer it flees to Olympus, the true dwelling of happiness."

No, Seneca is no help. But he is a fine example of the existence of Freud's Death Instinct, according to which the aim of all life is death, and the urge to return to an inanimate state[33].

The only wise remark in the opera wasn't made by Seneca. When Poppea's old nurse Arnalta vocalizes about the regrets of old age, a young lover, Valletto, jests that women reach the evening around noontime. Not so funny!

In the opera, Seneca is surrounded by friends and

relatives who grieve for him and movingly (in song) implore him, "Don't die, Seneca." It struck me that if I were in such a situation, not much of a crowd would hang around beseeching me not to die (even in prose). I haven't that many friends left. Seneca was pretty lucky in other ways, too. He was able to choose the time and method of his death.

Freud said[34] that is what everyone ultimately wants, to be able to choose his or her own method of dying, that the organism wishes to die only in its own fashion. That fashion is different for each of us, depending on what we value in life. My friend Kendall said she would be ready to die after her son married and had children. The artist Ruth Gaines has other values; she said, I want to paint one great painting before I die. A verse by Friedreich Holderlin[35] expresses similar sentiments:

A single summer grant me, great powers, and
A single autumn for fully ripened song
That, sated with the sweetness of my
Playing, my heart may more willingly die.

I know what he means. I would like to write one great book before I die. And then maybe, maybe, I'll be ready to go.

June 30

In recent years, I often worry about illness, certain that each stitch and pang is a harbinger of death. I'm reading a wonderful book, *One Hundred Over 100*, by Jim Heynen[36], of moments with a hundred North American centenarians. I am impressed with how beautiful and active many of the centurions still are, and how a goodly number continue to live alone. But most of all, I am struck by the many heart attacks, strokes, cancer operations, and diabetes the subjects have survived. Apparently despite their life threatening illnesses, they are determined not to die. It leaves me less frightened that I will die before I am ready. Don't worry so much about getting sick, I assure myself. It is not the absence of illness that keeps people alive; it is their fighting spirit.

One television program about people who lived past one hundred said that they had four things in common: a sense of humor, a slender physique, a deep involvement in some aspect of their lives, and had learned to accept loss. I immediately compared myself to these ancients, and decided to award myself a passing grade, if not an A, in all four aspects. All except the loss of life itself. I'll have to give myself an F- on that one.

Another TV commentator reported that there are now more than four thousand people over one hundred years old in the U.S. He added that the number is increasing yearly so that by the time the baby boomers grow up, there may be over one million centenarians in the country. I would love to help swell their ranks in the twenty-first century. If I do achieve the target age, I will feel fulfilled. But there is one good thing to say about not achieving that goal, however. Unlike a bad book review which twists my innards for days, if I fail to reach the bull's-eye I will never know about it.

Ronald Kotulak[37] brings some good news to Golden-Agers. (And what a laugh that expression is!) According to him, the common belief that the mind deteriorates as it ages is false, and scientists are finding there is not a lot of brain cell loss with advancing years. One researcher, K. Warren Schaie, compared twenty-five-year-old brains with those of seventy-five-year-olds and found there isn't much difference between the two groups. Keeping the mind active helps retain mental ability. Along with sex, the motto is, "Use it or lose it." Schaie says, "There are very few tottering, senile millionaires." According to him, seven factors predominate in oldsters who keep their mental prowess; above average education and income, a lack of chronic diseases, a willingness to change, marriage to a smart spouse, an ability to quickly grasp new ideas, and satisfaction with accomplishments.

Just as my teenager friends and I were obsessed with our physical development, and constantly compared breast, waist, and hip measurements, weight, and growth of pubic hair, I now study charts depicting decline in old age and contrast myself with their subjects. So where do I rate on Kotalak's list? In everything but marriage to a smart spouse I come out okay.

Further research indicates that although memory banks in the brains of many older people remain effective, some of their relay switches get dimmer, which explains why people tend to slow down as they grow older. This is another result of aging I find in myself. I sometimes am unable to think of a word, only to have it pop up in the middle of the next sentence. I am like a temperamental computer that takes a few moments to jump to the right spot. My memory is fine; it just takes longer to find it.

It seems we are all inclined to remember what concerns us the most. One of Stud Terkel's interviewees[38], a woman stockbroker of eighty-three, said, "In some ways I'm better than I was thirty-five years ago...My memory isn't so good on unimportant things. Where did I put my glasses? Where did I leave my keys? But if a customer asks me, 'do you remember what I paid for my IBM stock?' I remember right off the bat. I remember the birth dates of people I love." Cicero[39] in the first century B.C. said he certainly never heard of any old man forgetting where he had hidden his money.

The aged remember everything that interests them, their appointments to appear in court, and who are their creditors and who their debtors....Old men retain their mental faculties, provided their interest and application continue. This wisest of men, sounding like a member of the current fit generation, advised elders over two thousand years ago to adopt a regimen of health; to practice moderate exercise; and to take just enough food and drink to restore our strength and not to overburden it. Even greater care is required by the mind and soul, he continued, for they, too, like lamps, grow dim with time, unless we keep them supplied with oil.

Cicero then went on to describe the case of Sophocles, who was so involved in his literary work that he neglected his business affairs. His sons took him to court on the grounds of imbecility, hoping to remove him from the control of his property. Sophocles responded by reading his play, *Oedipus at Colonus*, which he had just written, and inquired if that sounded like the work of an imbecile. He was acquitted by the jury.

July 3

When James Stewart died last night, his imitator, Rich Little, said on TV, "It is not acceptable that Jimmy Stewart is dead. It was bad enough when he got old. But dead! That is unacceptable." My sentiments exactly. The old song, "Where have all the flowers gone?" swells up around me and pounds in my ears. All those wonderful movie stars gone forever, Charlie Chaplin, Spencer Tracy, Henry Fonda, James Cagney, Humphry Bogart, Robert Taylor, Tyrone Power, Jackie Gleason, Bette Davis, Joan Crawford, Barbara Stanwyck, Greer Garson, Lucille Ball. And now Jimmy Stewart. They weren't just actors to me; they were real live people who fueled my daily thinking. They were everything my parents, relatives, and teachers should have been and usually weren't. Before my eyes glowed weekly visions of beautiful people, exemplary lives, nobility, generosity, humor I still chuckle over (like Charlie Chaplin in the factory scene in Modern Times), and proof that true love exists. They taught me how to behave (I haven't missed making my own bed every morning since I read that Joan Crawford always made hers), how to dress, that dreams can come true. They demonstrated that good can triumph over evil, that justice can prevail. They were the kind of person I wanted to grow up to be, the originals who lived on for years in my fantasies. How empty the world seems without them! Fewer and fewer of them are left. When I first began writing this book, I believe Katherine Hepburn was the only one of the great stars still alive, and she was ill with Parkinson's. She has since died. It is the end of an era, with nothing to replace it, at least for me. Rich Little was right. It is not acceptable that Jimmy Stewart is dead.

Part 2: Science and Parapsychology

William James left a note when he died which said, "There are no answers. There are no conclusions." I hope he was wrong. I search everywhere for knowledge about death, for some words of wisdom or insight into human nature that will make letting go easier. In particular, I scrutinize books on science, where I hope to find ideas that will expand my thinking. Michio Kaku's *Hyperspace*[40] says that the essence of dialectics is that all objects, including people, gases, and the universe itself go through a series of changes. According to this philosophy, at each stage of development we face conflicts between two opposing forces. When the conflict is resolved we go on to the next level. Often small qualitative changes continue until they reach a breaking point and the object explodes.

At this phase of my life I am keeping a precarious balance between the longing to be at rest and the desire to live forever. According to Kaku's philosophy, I will go on fighting deterioration bit by bit for as long as I can, until one day the quantitative changes become qualitative, and all of a sudden I will die.

Nightmare: A middle-aged Alma is trying to shoot

me. She is agile and athletic in her body movements, and is wearing glasses. She aims her gun and I duck. She shoots again and again, and I hide behind a door and then crouch beneath a window. I dash in and out of stores and up and down alleys, with her shots barely missing me. She seems to get closer all the time. I wake up.

Illustration of Kaku's theory? Or does the dream mean that the middle-aged-Alma is working hard (so far successfully) at killing off the old lady? If so, old age is in pursuit and gaining all the time. Regardless, I'm glad I recorded the dream and believe I understand it. Shakespeare again[41]: "I find I seek to die, / And seeking death, find life."

I have been an atheist since my freshman year in college when we studied evolution in biology class. It seemed to me that evolution is a sensible explanation for how life developed that I thought eliminated the need to hypothesize the existence of God. But Kaku's book brings me second thoughts on the subject. Modern physics now speaks of universes with which we cannot communicate. Its findings suggest that in all likelihood other worlds exist beyond time and space. Scientists conclude that there are many dimensions beyond the four we know of, perhaps twenty-six, but are unable to enter yet. Who knows what is hidden in the other twenty-two? Maybe God is in one of them. When consciousness leaves our body, it is within the realm of possibility that it could enter one of the unknown dimensions. Einstein said matter never disappears, but simply reappears in another form. Wouldn't it be miraculous to find ourselves reappearing in one form or another after death? Shakespeare thought we would. He said, "What's past is prologue[42]." At this moment, that possibility doesn't sound any stranger than the findings of quantum theory. But since one has to die to find out, I am willing to settle for not knowing. I feel like Benjamin Franklin, who was asked on his deathbed if he thought there was an afterlife. He answered that he wasn't going to waste time speculating on the question, as he soon would find out first hand[43]. But still I continue my reading...

Modern physics, I've discovered, reduces all matters to mere shadows. Atoms are not considered things any longer, but particles of energy. Physicists conclude that on the atomic level the world of appearances ceases to exist. Sir James Jeans[44] summed it up thus: "The universe begins to look more like a great thought than like a great machine." Many scientists in frustration with the physics of today turn to parapsychology for answers.

I understand this movement well: if atoms basically are only shadows of the material world unknowable by human senses, who is to say that the dead cannot continue to exist on some atomic level as parcels of compressed energy, unseen, unfelt, and untouched by human beings?

For example, consider the ghostlike particle called the neutrino. It has no mass, no electrical charge, and no magnetic field. Traveling with the speed of light, it can glide through a planet such as earth as if it were empty space. This suggests that neutrinos occupy a special kind of space governed by different laws of nature, defining a different kind of space-time. Such discoveries encourage speculations about the existence of other particles which could provide the missing link between mind and matter, again leading to the possibility of survival after death.

I've always felt that creativity belongs outside the realm of psychology, and was excited to find that music also has been described as occupying the netherlands between spirit and matter. According to Heinrich Heine[45],

"Music is a strange thing. I would almost say it is a miracle. For it stands halfway between thought and phenomenon, between spirit and matter, a sort of nebulous mediator, like and unlike each of the things it mediates, spirit that requires manifestation in time and matter that can do without space.

We do not know what music is."

In my search for an extended life, I discovered that Jungian psychoanalyst Marie-Louise Von Franz believes there are scientific reasons for assuming the existence of life after death[46]. She says the architect Stefan von Jankovich, who survived a near-death experience, was considered clinically dead for twenty-three minutes. On returning to consciousness, he said that during his death he had discovered a primal energy, inexhaustible and timeless, continually radiating energy, absorbing energy and constantly pulsating. He believed that different worlds are formed from different oscillations, and therefore it is possible for separate worlds to exist simultaneously in the same place. Thus birth and death can be understood as events in which we pass from one oscillation frequency to another, and therefore enter another world.

According to Franz, Victor Solov had similar reflections, after coming close to death. He said he was moving swiftly toward a bright shining net which vibrated with a remarkable cold energy. The light increased to such intensity that it transformed him. He was transported into formlessness beyond time and space, not in another place but rather in another state of being. For him, too, spatial dimensions had been abolished.

Franz[47] said that Jung never got tired of stressing that a certain part of the psyche is not bound to the space-time category. He maintained that the dead communicate with live human beings by utilizing the physiology (sympathetic nervous system) of the living.

I had a strange experience that gives credence to Jung's explanation of how the dead communicate with us. I was driving to my daughter's house in the sleeting rain caused by the fever bands of Hurricane Lily, which I was trying to escape. The night was pitch-black and the torrential rainstorm continued for hours. I drove on and on, although I could barely see a few feet ahead of me. Terrified and exhausted, I wondered if I should exit the turnpike and search for a hotel in the dark, flooded side roads.

"What should I do, Rudy?" I asked my dead husband.

"Keep driving!" he said, in the direct way he had. Communication through my sympathetic nervous system? I have no idea. I only know that I took his advice and arrived safely at my destination.

Rosalind Heywood finds a further rationale for the existence of life after death[48]. She speaks of meeting a friend who had recently died and was resuscitated, who said he now had scope and opportunity beyond his wildest dreams. When she asked for evidence of his liberation, he responded,

42

"I can't give you any evidence. You have no concepts for these conditions. I can only give you poetic images."

Heywood also writes of Dr. Richard Gregory's suggestion[49] that travelers in space might be faced with a similar problem. If we were to meet a new kind of life form, Gregory suspects we could not be able to recognize it. "The perceptual system is a computer," he writes, "programmed by evolutionary experience and by our own personal experience of the world. A new kind of object requires the perceptual computer to solve a new problem with an old programme, which may be neither adequate nor appropriate."

Perhaps there are dead souls all around us, and we are unable to see them because of our sensual limitations. What an exciting thought! A warm glow blankets my heart at the (faint) possibility that I am surrounded by Rudy, Joan, Anna, Jill, and Kendall, even if I can't see or hear them.

Another idea of dead souls makes a great deal of sense. My mother said at the end of her life that even though she was old, she felt exactly the same inside as when she was a child. I feel the same way, as though there is a continuity of *Alma-ness*, in which a thread winds through my life from my earliest days to the present like a string of pearls. The five-year-old Alma who mourned her pet Easter chick still exists in the aging lady who is trying to understand mortality. George Orwell once said that a nation has the power to change beyond recognition, and yet remain essentially the same. So it is with us human beings. I sensed this from the time I was seven years old, when I sat in front of the *Books of Knowledge* and thought, of all ages, this one is the most me. The feeling of self remains fixed, whatever the age of the individual or the severity of his or her illness. Indeed, the self feels independent of the body altogether. Might it not be true, then, that even when the self leaves the body permanently it continues to exist on its own? If so, it is only another step upward in the consistency of selfhood.

I was sitting by my mother's side at the moment she died. Something seemed to have gone out of her. She looked the same, yet somehow utterly different, emptier, perhaps, or even diminished in size. I've had the same sensation on viewing a body at a funeral, as if the corpse is physically smaller than when alive. When I read somewhere that immediately after dying people weigh less than a few moments before, I remembered the feeling I'd had at my mother's deathbed. Something *did* go out of her to make her weigh less. Could it have been her soul?

Heartened as I am by this kind of thinking, I remain essentially unconvinced. Like Shakespeare[50], I say, "O Time, thou must untangle this, not I, / It is too hard a knot for me t'untie."

But be there life after death or not, I determine, like the High Lama of Shangri-La, to make every effort to see that my final conflict on earth lasts as long as possible. I think of the High Lama a lot; *Lost Horizon* has been my favorite film since I was sixteen years old. I see it over and over, each time it is brought back to the theatres.

In the film, a plane carrying a group of travelers crashes near the inaccessible Himalayan Utopia. The survivors are led by a rescue party to Shangri-La, where they find perfect climate, peaceful inhabitants, perennial flowers, perpetually singing birds, a glorious castle containing in its archives all the art and literature of the world, and the two-hundred-year-old High Lama who wishes to hand over his mantle to Ronald Coleman. All the passengers find peace and fulfillment in the land of perpetual summer, where age is greatly retarded and time itself is slowed up. What I remember most in the film is Margo, who talks Coleman's party into leaving the utopia. As she passes over the mountains which protect Shangri-La from the elements and fights her way through the windswept ice and snow of the Himalayas, she ages by fifty years, the time she has lived in Shangri-La, and dies. I was haunted by the sight of Margo instantly transformed from a lovely young woman into an ancient hag. The image has occurred to me time and again during the fifty-seven years that have elapsed since my first viewing of the film. I think it would be just as horrible and equally incredible if any young woman were to get a sudden look at how she would look fifty years hence, wrinkles and all.

I recently found myself remembering a company of actors with whom I played summer stock in a small New Hampshire village years ago. It was a beautiful young troop-none of us could have been more than twenty-five years old. Suddenly, abracadabra! Graceful Mary, poised Sidnee, talented Jean, gentle Reino, virile Henry, and dignified Earl were transmogrified into drab old men and women. People remain eternally young in our unconscious. To take them out and view them in the light of day freezes the blood.

Of course *Lost Horizon* is my favorite film. The High Lama lives to be two hundred years old, and doesn't die until he decides the time is right. Everyone else remains ageless. And all you have to do to keep from getting old is to live in paradise.

Leos Janacek's opera, *The Metropoulos Case,* in which Elina Makropoulos is three hundred thirty-seven years old, tells a different story. The tale goes back to the rule of Rudolf 11, the last Hapsburg Emperor and King of Bohemia. Rudolf commanded a court physician to devise a potion that would give the Emperor another three hundred years of life. He then ordered the physician to try the potion first on his sixteen-year-old daughter, Elina. The Emperor did not take the potion. As Elina pointed out three hundred years later, how could he know it would work? She escaped, taking with her the document which contained the secret formula. With centuries to perfect her technique, she became one of the greatest singers of all time. (Oh, to live three hundred thirty-seven years, if for that reason alone!) But she had seen so many lives and deaths that she lost all interest in the people around her. Fearing her death was imminent, she returned to Prague to seek the Metropoulos document, hoping to give herself three hundred more years of life. When the signs of death were upon her, she recovered the document. But realizing in her last moments that her life had already been too long and unhappy, she found that she envied ordinary mortals whose brief lives make values and meaning possible. She died without taking the potion, as she watched the secret formula go up in flames. Not I! Alma Metropoulos would have taken the secret potion.

When Jonathan Swift's Lemuel Gulliver visited the country of the Struldbruggs in the neglected Third Voyage of *Gulliver's Travels*[51], he encountered a reaction similar to Elina's on her deathbed. When Gulliver first arrived, he was captivated by the idea that the inhabitants lived forever, but was soon disenchanted. Gulliver found them the most mortifying sight he ever beheld. For by the time the Struldbruggs reached the age of eighty, most of them were so removed from pleasure they felt melancholy and dejected and were dead to natural affection. In their nineties, they were so senile they could neither hold a conversation nor read a book. At best, they could look forward to an eternity of envy and impotent desires.

I question that all eighty year olds become melancholy and dejected! Dr. Margaret Ray (age eighty-three), and my sister, Pauline Stein (age eighty-one), remain as interested in life as ever. And my Uncle Emil, who lived to be ninety-seven, found a new lover at the age of ninety-three and continued to edit the newspaper of the retirement home where he lived until he died.

Swift's Third Voyage is commonly regarded as his own views on the hideousness of old age. Book Three foreshadowed his own declining years, which were darkened by loneliness and dread of insanity. He spiraled through a period of increasing mental illness and died at the age of seventy-eight. Perhaps someone should have said to the noted satirist, Speak for yourself, Dr. Swift!

Part 3: Jung's Hypothesis of Life after Death

July 28

I pooh-poohed Jung's hypothesis of the dear departed communicating with survivors through their sympathetic nervous systems until a memory of my brother's death made Jung's thinking seem plausible.

Zane (for whom my son was named) had applied to become a midshipman in the Navy during World War 11, but was rejected because he was so nearsighted. It seems to me the disappointment was too great for him to bear, and in fact was great enough to kill him.

One morning he came downstairs and said, "I've got a headache." I was upset. He hardly ever had headaches. But I didn't want to worry him and said lightly, "Take a couple of aspirins."

He said, "I did before I went to bed and I still woke up with a headache." Since he was my little brother whom I had always taken care of, he asked me my advice.

I told him to go to the doctor right away. He had met a young doctor in the local ice cream parlor where he went for sodas and he liked him. Zane said he decided he would go see him. A half hour later he returned, saying, "The doctor said if I had a headache that bad I have to go to bed."

The doctor told our mother and father that he saw an obstruction he suspected was an abscess behind Zane's eye. Our parents panicked and immediately switched to another doctor. He diagnosed a bad case of the flu, a diagnosis that was more to everybody's liking.

Zane stayed in bed with violent headaches. He remained under the doctor's care for two weeks until even the doctor panicked, and sent Zane to the hospital by ambulance. The first physician had been right on target. There *was* an obstruction behind Zane's eye. An abscess had spread to his brain.

They took him out feet first to the ambulance. Our mother became hysterical. She said that was the way they carried dead bodies out of the house.

Our hopes were high every day before going to the hospital to visit him. We would troop in enthusiastically, feeling that "Today is the day he will be better!" But each day we were frightened to see him lose ground.

A brain surgeon operated on him three different times. The third time he died under the knife. They brought him back to life-for a few hours. The last time he was conscious he had a defeated look in his eyes. I said, "Zaney, honey, you have a tough fight. Are you fighting?" He shook his head.

Zane suffered horribly for those three weeks in the hospital. The pus had so invaded his skull that his eye stuck out like a grapefruit. He had lost his speech by then and all night long cried out, "Nus, nus, nus!" The family thought he was calling for the nurse, but we'll never know for sure.

One day we would see him and he looked a little better, perhaps even sitting up in bed. The next day he was delirious with pain. On one of the times he seemed to be recovering, my Aunt Mary walked into his room and started screaming. I thought, what's the matter with her? Can't she see he is better! Of course Mary was right. Zane died shortly thereafter.

What a tragedy for my parents. The hospital called at four in the morning to tell them to come right away. Pauline had come home with her baby, Susan, to be with our brother. Father was pulling up his pants to get ready, and Mother uncharacteristically screamed at him for taking so long. He didn't seem to mind, for he understood her feelings.

The three of them left for the hospital. I had offered to stay home to take care of the baby. I sat there glassy eyed, waiting, waiting. I knew with certainty Zane had died. Baby Susan awakened with a smile and received in return what must have been a ghastly grimace. My family left in the dark and returned to the light of day.

I tried to comfort my mother, although we had never been close. She said she didn't want to live anymore. I said, "You have to live, Mother. You have two other children who need you." It didn't help. Then I said, "Mother, you believe in God. You will see Zane in Heaven."

My mother shrieked, "It's not enough! My heart is broke! My heart is broke!"

When she said she didn't want to live, she meant it. She died shortly thereafter of a cerebral hemorrhage. Father followed her a few years later.

A few hours after Zane's death, I had a strange experience. It seemed my brother's presence was floating somewhere near the ceiling above me. His voice permeated the entire room.

Tell Mother I couldn't wait anymore. I'm sorry I'm making all of you unhappy. I love you. Be comforted now, I'm very happy. I know everything. I'm part of everything. It's wonderful. Don't grieve for me. This is where I want to be.

This was so profound an experience that I immediately wrote down the words. Then I read them to the congregation at the funeral. As I spoke, a collective gasp arose from the mourners and seemed to fill the room.

He was eighteen years old, a beautiful young man. His death was the greatest tragedy of my life. I wanted to die in his place; I had my college ring buried in his coffin instead. When we lost my brother we lost the whole family along with him. Zane was the only male descendent of our family. There is no one left now to carry on our father's name. And there is the empty space left in our lives by the family he would have had. With his death went a potential wife and children, an uncle and aunt and the cousins my children never had.

It nearly destroyed us all. We lost interest in living. I obsessed: what is it all about? What is the sense? For the first time I realized that our lives hang by a thread, that a hairline exists between life and death, that we are all only a heartbeat away from death and disaster. One moment he was alive and the next he was gone. How easily we pass over that line.

There are many things I can never forgive myself for. Before he went to the hospital he had to stay in bed in a darkened room with his horrible headaches. But he was lonely and wanted me to sit with him. I was listening to music on the radio and wanted to continue, but the sound hurt his head. I told him if I could listen to the music I would stay in the room. So he agreed. Now I can't bear the thought that I subjected him to that additional pain.

But what I forgive myself for least of all is the knowledge that I allowed my parents to heed the words of the second doctor and deny the ghastly diagnosis of the first doctor. After all, I was more educated. I should have had more distance; I should have insisted he be tested further and not go along with their denial. Then the abscess might have been discovered in time, and he would be alive today.

Partly in reparation, I returned to school to study psychology and psychoanalysis. Until recent years, I devoted most of my life to curing sick brains. I couldn't help my brother but I have helped many others instead. Perhaps his death was not altogether in vain.

Part 4: The Death Book, Maybe.

August 1

Each loss brings back previous losses. The recollection of Zane's death reawakened memories of my friends which I had managed to submerge. Waiting to board a plane to visit Janet, I sat drinking coffee in the airport restaurant. As I sipped, I idly recalled that two of my present friends ordered only water with their meals. I wondered why, and then mused that both women were hardy New England Presbyterian types with Scottish ancestry, who didn't believe in indulging themselves. Then I tried to remember what my dead friends had drunk with their meals. What wouldn't I give to have even a glass of water now with any one of them, I thought with fogged up eyes.

I fantasied that Jill was sitting with me in the restaurant. What would she have ordered? Probably water. Anna would have ordered a coke, and Kendall habitually ordered not one, but two glasses of cranberry juice. And what did Joan order? My eyes teared over when I realized that I couldn't remember.

Joan was like an exotic bird, I thought with a smile, Jill, a gentle sea breeze who could suddenly become a

51

hurricane, Anna a classic wife and mother, and Kendall-Kendall was of a breed unlike anyone on earth.

Useless bits and pieces of conversations with my friends stuck in my bowels like pieces of shrapnel. Anna had said she found Dove easier on her skin than other soaps, Jill told me that some people ate only the bulbs of scallions and threw away the green part, while Kendall put the knives in her dishwasher bottom side up so they would get cleaner during the wash. Images drilled into my mind so shrilly that I cupped my hands over my ears. What difference does it make if Kendall always put the roll of toilet paper in backwards? In self defense I wondered if recasting the obsessive thoughts into a novel would wrench them out.

I dreamed I had to go to the ladies' room. I went into a ratty, tinny old bathroom, the kind that once was found in old movie houses. The doors to the stalls were open and wouldn't shut. There were no toilets in them. The only complete one was locked. I woke up realizing that I never got to use the facilities.

Is my death journal a good idea? I don't know if anyone under AARP age would find it interesting. Maybe I'll be more depressed if I write it. Elina Metropoulos might have had the right idea. The ostrich approach at least makes your daily life endurable.

I sent an Email to my dear friend, Dr. Mary Bruce, a poet and professor of Literature at Monmouth College, Monmouth, Illinois, asking what she thought about the idea. Mary answered:
"The death journal is your best idea yet. In fact, it may be the source of your immortality, since I am certain it will find a ready market."

"But Mary," I protested back, "I don't know anything about dying! How could I? Like Philip Kane, I've never died. Dr. George Sheehan[52], the great running guru and writer, said in his last book that you shouldn't write about a marathon unless you've run it, and you shouldn't write about cancer unless you've got it. And you shouldn't write about death unless you're dying.

"Well, I know a little bit about aging because I'm doing it, and I know something of the fear of dying because

I've got it. But for me, like Sheehan, writing the epilogue will be the problem."

Mary answered, "Never mind, dear. Death is as taboo in our age as sex was in Freud's. You will learn a lot of things as you write, as well as be the usual spiritual life-giver you always are."

Me, spiritual? I laughed. Mary must have forgotten I'm an atheist! Nevertheless, I was thrilled at her reaction to my idea for a book. In rereading Thomas Mann's *The Magic Mountain*[53], one of my favorite books of all time, I was delighted to come across a passage which bore out Mary's thinking.

The young hero, Hans Castorp, is convalescing at a sanatorium for consumptives. One of the guests has died. Castorp tried to introduce the subject of death at the dinner table:

"but was met with such a flat and callous rebuff on all sides... Frau Stohl had been downright gruff. What did he mean by introducing such a subject- what kind of upbringing had he had? The house regulations protected the patients from having such things come to their knowledge; and now here was a young whippersnapper bringing it up at table... If it happened again she would complain."

It seems to me that things have not changed much on that score since the book was first published in 1924. Mary's message left me refreshed and encouraged, and I determined to proceed with the book. In fact, I have no choice but to continue, as I believe the only alternative to the death journal is death itself.

My spirits were also lifted when my granddaughter Rachel phoned to ask if I knew the words to *The Battle Hymn of the Republic,* an assignment given to her in school. Her parents had no idea of the words. I, who had fought my way through it for years in grammar school assembly, started singing the song to Rachel. I got as far as "He is trampling out the vintage where the grapes of wrath are stored" when I got stuck. Rachel is only eight years old, and had never asked me to do anything like that before. I couldn't disappoint her, but could think of nobody who would remember the song. Certainly my irreligious children wouldn't. Jill might have, but she was dead. What to do? Suddenly a delightful thought came to my rescue. I phoned the public library, where the pleasant reference librarian found the hymn and read me the line. I quickly called Rachel and sang, 'He hath loosed the fateful lightening of his terrible swift sword.' The child was ecstatic. I fantasized that fifty years from now Rachel would think, "My grandmother could always be depended on."

I haven't experienced much pleasure since Shirley's death because I've been in mourning for my friends and my own mortality. This morning, much to my surprise, the rays of sunlight streaming into my bedroom felt warm on my face. I lifted it up to the sun and stretched. The lock of hair blown on my forehead danced in the breeze. Birdsong delighted my ears, and in the Catholic school yard next door the branches of the Flame tree hung heavy with orange enchantment. The brilliant magentas, mint greens, and banana yellows of the bromeliads in my back yard dazzled my eyes, while the scent of frangipani blew in from the garden until my lungs expanded with sweetness. For the first time in months I cooked myself a decent dinner and thought life isn't so bad after all. I'm lucky to have a wonderful friend like Mary left to me, and a beautiful caring family. I love my pretty little house. I enjoy living here in eternal summer where the scent of flowers perpetually lifts me to heaven. Who needs Shangri-La when one can live in Key West? I had all but forgotten what a good cook I can be when I work at it and how much I enjoy a good meal. The shrimp creole tasted delicious with a glass of Zinfandel. And I didn't even mind cleaning up. I think I'll ask June over tomorrow night to help finish the shrimp.

That evening I sat down at my computer and typed SHIRLEY SYMS, the name of the first of my five friends to die.

Part 5: Shirley Syms* is Calling Me

August 15

"Alma, Alma," Shirley called. Night after night, as soon as I closed my eyes, her soft, musical voice bid me come.

Shirley Syms died of breast cancer. She was the first of my five friends to die. We weren't intimate friends, but rather had what I felt was a friendship waiting to happen. I liked and admired her, enjoyed our encounters, and suspected that we could eventually become close friends. Shirley's manner was cool and off putting, as if she needed several feet of space between her and the rest of the world. People who are difficult to get to know well are a challenge when I like them, for when they open up, they can become friends for life. Some of my most cherished friendships began in such an inauspicious way. But I failed to penetrate the guarded layers of Shirley's psyche. I know she liked me, and until I left New York we continued to meet occasionally. But the relationship never deepened beyond our first few meetings. I felt Shirley and I had unfinished business.

---

* Certain features of Mrs. Syms' life have been changed to disguise her true identity.

55

The first dream came right before she died. As soon as I opened my eyes I knew she was dying. But why was she calling me? Why did she want me to go with her? I didn't know her that well. Was she sorry we never got to know each other better?

In the dream, Shirley's voice was light, happy, and playful. Not at all as if she were sad about dying. It was as if she were saying:

Join me, Alma. There are grape arbors here, with purple grapes so huge you'd think they were plums, and wonderful luminescent blossoms that light up the air like the sunrise, a sweet perfume that no winds can scatter fills the air. Soft music like "Lohengrin" is wafted by gentle breezes. Here you are separated from your body and can float high above the flower of peace, the Rose that cannot wither. In this kingdom no person is king, and no one a subject. You don't have to think at all, Alma; you simply understand everything there is to know. Everybody and everything is here all at once. It is eternity, and I am in the middle of it. Come now, Alma. It is foolish to wait.

I felt a fleeting pang of envy. Shirley was leaving this world of sorrow and misfortune for an infinitely grander existence.

Shortly thereafter I dreamed:

I was wandering high up on a hill over a river (the River Styx?). I looked down and saw that the water was a raging ocean. I was terrified and slowly slid down the hill on my buttocks. I thought, If I close my eyes and don't look down I won't be so scared.

To me the dream said if you don't look at the terrors of the aging process, it isn't so scary.

Easier dreamed than done, I thought, as I remembered a stanza in Alfred Lord Tennyson's *In Memoriam* I had memorized in high school:

So runs my dream: but what am I?
An infant crying in the night:
An infant crying for the light:
And with no language but a cry[54].

Tennyson was onto something. Here I was seventy years old. One by one the pleasures of life were dwindling away. With heightened cholesterol worries, my dietary delights shrink yearly. When my husband died, he took sex with him. And since the death of my dear friends, life had become one long tunnel of grief. Their loss had diminished me, as though they had taken part of me along with them. I felt as Shakespeare's Cleopatra did when Anthony died, There is nothing left remarkable/ Beneath the visiting moon[55].

The third dream: I am walking with a family on a beautiful high cliff overlooking the ocean. I look down and the ocean is dazzling. I had been swimming there before. A handsome boy mutters that we cannot go swimming now. I say sadly, "That's too bad. I have gone swimming all over the world, and one of the most beautiful swims I have ever had was right here."

My husband and I had walked along such beautiful ocean scenes many times in our travels around the world. Yes, I believed those beautiful swimming days were gone forever. They were a sublime part of my life and I grieved for them. The boy was not interested in swimming with me, and I doubted if anyone I wanted ever would be again.

The analyst Theodore Reik once told me, "In the end there is only work[56]." Unfortunately, except for the occasional winsome presence of my children and grandchildren, my sentiments were closer to DeGaulle's "Old age is a shipwreck." Then I dreamed.

A clock only lasts fifty years. The clock is large and round, the kind that used to hang in old school rooms, and is outlined in black.

I decided this was my biological clock, which now was defined by grief, that I've outstayed my welcome by almost a quarter of a century.

Suddenly I realized that the clock also stands for sex, as did the ocean in the previous dream, and I was in mourning for its loss. Life's delights are as fleeting as tiny balls of mercury. If people understood this, not a single one would be allowed to escape. How many say to an amorous mate, "Wait until this program is over?" And how few of those programs do they remember fifty years later. I'm proud I wasn't one of those who prefer TV (talking, eating,

57

reading, etc.) to sex.

In the dream Shirley asked, "Shouldn't one think about that time span when buying a clock?"

Yes, indeed, Shirley, the clock should remind us that our life span is relentlessly ticking away.

The dream confirms that our lives are shaped and controlled by the movements of the clock. When we are born and when we die, who in the vast stretch of history becomes our relatives and friends, when we eat, sleep, make love, and work, if and what we read and write, what we know and what we learn; indeed there is no aspect of our lives that is not structured within the confines of time.

I traveled to Europe for the first time when I was forty years old. The trip was a gift from my actor husband, in appreciation for my allowing him to go on the road in *Fiorello*. He was going to stay home with the children while I was away. Although I wanted badly to see Europe, I was reluctant to leave twelve-year-old Zane, and Janet and Jonathan, the five-year-old twins.

I enjoyed most of the trip, and even managed to squelch my anxiety part of the time. But the night before my flight home, I lay in bed clutching the bed covers, staring out the white-curtained window at the Eiffel Tower. I thought, I'll climb to the top of the Tower and jump off. Then *I'll* be in charge of my life and won't have to worry about the plane crashing and never seeing my children again. I want to leave those I love when I decide to, not at the erratic twirl of the wheel of fate. The clock will determine when I am to die. If I join Shirley now, I will be in command. That is the only way I know to beat the clock. But if controlling destiny is what I want, why do I wake up in anxiety after the Shirley dreams?

Shirley Syms was a lady, an elegant woman, always dressed in the latest designer fashions. When her son was married at the Plaza, she moved down the aisle in her golden Givenchy gown with the grace of a queen born to the crown. She had spent her life setting the stage and creating a beautiful comfortable home for her husband, the great surgeon, Timothy Syms. Even before Shirley and I met, I had enjoyed reading about the Syms in the society columns. They were philanthropists, and, as a doctor's wife, she chaired and served on committees for Mt. Sinai Hospital and charity benefits. It struck me even then that she never seemed to serve twice on the same board. She later told me she had also tried various careers, bridge player and teacher, interior designer, landscape gardener, realtor, all of which she did flawlessly. But one by one she shrugged them aside. She puzzled me. Who *was* Shirley Syms? I sensed that the elegant lady of the Social Register concealed a confused little girl.

We had met at our health club on Eighty-Sixth Street in New York, and then sometimes lunched together on the sunshine-doused terrace of the club. But much as I enjoyed Shirley's company, she continued to hold me at a distance, permitting our friendship to go only so far and no further.

I met her at the health club after her first chemotherapy session. She looked stunning as ever in her stylishly-cut blond wig, her regal posture and cultivated demeanor radiating poise. No one ever would have suspected she was ill. To my surprise, she quietly told me about her cancer, and said she was fighting it hard and doing everything she could to get well. Moved that she'd confided in me, I said if I ever got cancer, I hoped I would handle it exactly as she was doing.

That was the last time I saw her. A few months later I read her obituary in the *New York Times*.

Shortly thereafter, a neighbor told me Jerry Smeltzer was dead. Jerry in early middle age was surrounded by loving friends. He had inherited a lot of money, and didn't need to work. He spent his time reading, traveling, and going to art exhibits. Many people envied him and thought he had an idyllic life. I wasn't so sure. He didn't seem to care passionately about any one thing. His story sounded suspiciously like Shirley's and Anna's, who seemed to have wonderful existences, but apparently not good enough to keep them alive. I believe that to stay in this life you have to *want* something with all your heart and soul.

Deepak Chopra[57], the successful physician and best selling author, expresses similar sentiments. In speaking of his own life, he says, "Every new day has to mean something to me, and if it does, I believe the battle is won."

59

For hundreds of years, the connection between physical illness and emotions has been suspected. Now science has unearthed substantial evidence for its existence. Indeed, studies show that a certain type of personality is characteristic of cancer patients. According to Fritjof Capra[58], Carl Simonton and Stephanie Matthews-Simonton have developed a psychosomatic model of cancer that demonstrates how psychological and physical states work together in the onset of the disease. Lawrence LeShan, in his study of more than five hundred cancer patients, found similar components in their life histories. Particularly important in the personalities of these individuals is that they internalized despair and were unable to let others know when they felt hurt, angry, or hostile. In my opinion, this personality trait was characteristic of both Shirley and Anna, whose deeper selves were buried under socially approved masks.

An old Polish proverb says, "When a girl becomes a wife, she is buried alive[59]." In my opinion, that proverb tells the story of the life and death of these two women, who buried themselves in the lives of their husbands.

Two nights after my meeting with Shirley, I had another dream about her.

This time, as she called, a man is opening a bank card, and is given a pin number so he can withdraw money from the cash machine. He demands to know what it means to have a pin number and who is the supervisor.

To understand a dream fully, the dreamer must freely associate to each detail of the dream. This means that for the purposes of the dream he or she must accept without censorship the first thing that comes to mind. In this way, the underlying message of the dream becomes clear. Withdrawing money from the cash machine made me think of using up the days that are remaining to me. When I associated to pin number, I wondered how much time was left in my lifetime account. Is my life span genetically determined, is it decided by some higher being, by Fate, or, as I would like to believe, am I the supervisor of my life? It had never before occurred to me to ask such questions about the meaning of death. My only reflections on the subject were to protest it. Life gets sweeter as I get older. I don't want to go gentle into that good night. I'll go out kicking, screaming, cursing, if at all. I love it here; I hate it there. I'm not going!

What, me, die? So soon? Such a thing is not possible. Everybody has to die sometime. Of course they do. Certainly. Only a fool would deny that. But *me*? No, the thought is only a nightmare. I'll wake up any moment now in the arms of my love.

Shakespeare, the wisest of us all, agrees that I don't have to go, that it is unnecessary to yield to old age except in surrender to hatred of one's adversaries. Edgar in *King Lear* says, "World, world, O world! / But that thy strange mutations make us hate thee/ Life would not yield to age[60]." I don't hate anyone or anything that much, expect perhaps death itself.

Of course not everyone feels the way I do. Carl Jung[61] says, "There are people who feel no craving for immortality, and who shudder at the thought of sitting on a cloud and playing the harp for ten thousand years!" Although I, too, have some reservations about the desirability of eternal harp playing, I am thankful I don't share that kind of thinking.

In contrast, I love the *New Yorker* cartoon[62] in which the doctor standing beside a patient in a hospital bed says, "He's one tough cookie. I've never seen anyone bounce back from an autopsy before."

I'm like my grandfather, a spry, slender man who walked miles every day well into his nineties, a half century before the fitness craze inundated America. He used to eat a hard boiled egg in a white egg cup for lunch, cutting off one slice at a time with his pocket knife.

Once when I was twelve, and we were sitting on his neatly painted gray porch, he told me he didn't want to die.

"You've had a wonderful life and are a very old man, Grandfather," I said. "Isn't that enough?"

"If you ate yesterday, don't you want to eat today?" he answered.

Throughout the bank card dream, Shirley's voice kept calling, "Alma, Alma..." It grew louder and louder until it escalated into a shriek that blasted my eardrums. It seemed so real I couldn't believe she wasn't actually there. The dream had an uncanny feeling about it as if in some unknown time and place I had been there before. I was terrified I would follow her.

I woke up furious at Shirley. I'd had enough of her calls. They were too real for comfort. "Shut up, Shirley. Shut up!" I shouted, holding my hands over my ears. "Get out of my head. It's not my fault we never got to be closer friends. I can't help it that you aren't around any more. I'm sorry, but I don't want to know you badly enough to die for it. I'll join you when I'm good and ready, not when *you* want me to!"

And that was that, for my dreams about Shirley Syms.

Part 6: Joan Simonton

August 30

When we met, Joan Simonton was a sexy girl, a teen-aged Sophia Loren. When she got older, she looked like a middle-aged Sophia Loren. My eyes filled with tears when I saw *Grumpier Old Men*, because it brought Joan back in the flesh. Sophia is aging well. Joan had, too. She had a voluptuous figure and luxurious black hair twice the size of her face, so you never noticed that her nose was too long. She wore tight skirts and low cut dresses, and swung her hips when she walked. You could smell her perfume before she entered the room. Some women who look and act sexy are really hysterics and duds in the bedroom. But not Joan. Her sex life was full and rich and gave her a lifetime of pleasure. Joan's zest for living made even a chance encounter exciting. Looking at a painting with her was an emotional experience. When she saw the portrait of a sad faced Haitian woman in my office, she cried. I never look at that painting without thinking of Joan. She had a delightful sense of humor and laughed with pleasure as she once imagined and described an encounter between me and a fantasy lover. She wasn't far off the mark.

Joan was the daughter of a well-off, rather gruff,

manufacturer of watchbands, and a beautiful, ladylike mother. She had one older and one younger brother, both far better looking children than their once scrawny, big-beaked sister. She was the niece of a famous Hollywood producer, who was so esteemed by the family that Joan decided when she grew up she would become a movie star, perhaps thinking she would gain the adulation her handsome brothers received.

We became friends when we were fifteen years old and members of The Cosmopolitan Theatre Guild. Since at fifteen we were its stars, it's not hard to imagine the quality of the productions. I played the lead in the solitary performance of *God and the Empress*, memorable only for the crown's slipping down over my eyes, which I then couldn't get off. Joan played my daughter, and was as exciting an actress as she was a person. Chills still ripple down my back as I remember her musical, lilting voice declaiming, "My country? My country? I don't care about my country. Why should I care about it? It never cared about me." The cast sold punch board chances for tickets with the number punched determining the price paid for admission. After seeing *God and the Empress* a friend who had picked a chance costing one cent, said it wasn't worth a penny more.

At the demise of the infamous Cosmopolitan, Joan and I joined the Neighborhood Players, where she was cast as the consumptive Camille. Chubbier than Joan, I asked Julie Sutton, the director, if I could try out for the role, too. She smiled, and said, "No, dear." While Joan hacked away, I did a lot of ushering.

Joan, the partner of my theatrical career. I smile when I picture two intense teenagers daydreaming over geometry books about how they were going to become great actresses. The fantasy filled our lives for a decade, and then bit by bit got absorbed into the fabric of our daily lives.

For forty years Joan and I met on and off to share news about our careers and then our families. Her husband, Frank, had been table tennis champion of Vienna when he was a young man. His mother was a dentist long before women had careers. When Joan married Frank, he earned his living blowing beautiful glass sculptures. I loved to watch him shaping the liquefied glass into delicate patterns and forms, which slowly became recognizable as *objects d'art*. I still treasure the intricate lions, tigers, and ships he created for me.

Joan, Frank, Rudy, and I spent every New Year's Eve together for almost twenty years. We lived our youth together. We raised our children together. Never a New Year's Eve goes by that I don't remember our parties.

Frank was fifty-five years old when Joan quietly told me he was going to die. He was driving his dilapidated Chevy, with Joan in the passenger's seat and Rudy and me in the back. Joan said Frank had leukemia.

I didn't think I heard her correctly, and strained forward until my chin touched the front seat. "He's going to be all right, isn't he?" Joan slowly shook her head.

I was numb. I couldn't absorb her meaning. People our age simply did not die. Frank was the first person to die in my life since my brother Zane died when I was twenty-one. Two decades had passed, and I had learned nothing to help me accept the concept of death.

Frank was not an intimate friend, but for months after he died I was bewildered and depressed. At times I still am. There are certain truths that don't sink in for decades, if ever.

After Frank's death Joan said she went around the world with only her tennis racket for company and was never lonely. Whatever country she was visiting, she could always find partners for a game. But Joan would have made friends wherever she was, with or without her tennis racket.

A few years later, Joan married Seymour Smith, a jovial realtor with whom she seemed well mated and happy. Joan and I used to have a lot of fun together giggling about life and sex. Between her marriages, Joan met a married man she liked, and they had sex together in a quaint motel upstate. Every year after that, as in the movie, *This Time Next Year*, she and the man met at the motel and repeated their liaison. According to Joan, Seymour never knew.

Speaking of Seymour, a chubby, pleasant, thoroughly nice man who was a good husband to Joan, I wondered what kind of mate he would make for me. No chemistry, I decided, and put the thought aside.

Joan was a unique woman in many ways, but most of all for the kind of mother she was.

Her muscular, handsome son Algy was in college when he asked her, "What would you say if I told you I was in love with a guy?" Joan gulped and decided to treat Algy's question as a joke. Nothing further was said about his question until years later, when Algy brought his doctor lover home. This time Joan no longer could swallow the truth. She telephoned her son later and blasted him, "How can you do this to me? You see a psychiatrist or you can forget you have a mother!" There was silence at the other end of the phone. Algy had hung up.

Several months passed with no contact between them. Then one day, he called. "Hi, Mom," he said. "Are you still my mother?"

Joan crumbled. They had always been close, and she knew she could never reject her son.

"Well, Mom, are you there?" he persisted.

"Yes, dear," she answered. "Of course I'm still your mother. Nothing can ever change that."

Though devastated, Joan loved him dearly and determined to do something about her reaction. In her fifties, she returned to graduate school to work for a master's degree in social work. She searched vainly for a small intimate group led by a trained therapist who understood homosexuality, and came to realize there must be millions who had such a family member and were in need of a place where they could meet under the auspices of a respected and recognized institution.

One day, she was struck by the idea that was to change her life and that of countless others: her research topic would be to invade the privacy of despairing parents of gays and find out how they were coping. They would share a huge crying towel, give vent to their pain and desperation together, and try to overcome their feelings of prejudice.

She sought out more than sixty-five parents of gays and began leading workshops for them. After receiving a degree in social work she became a counselor to these families, and wrote her beautiful, passionate book, "Are You

Still My Mother?[63]"

Despite her great work, Joan had relapses, such as when she first saw Algy and his lover kiss each other good morning. And when Algy called his lover dear, Joan thought, "Dear? To a man?" She told me that coming to terms with gay children was a never-ending battle. But her sense of fairness and love for Algy always managed to overcome her prejudice. When I last saw Algy, at Joan's funeral, he said proudly, "I'm lucky she was my mom."

Joan became proud of Algy, too. At thirty-three years, he was a licensed psychiatrist, director of a successful urban private practice, and Chairman for the Committee on Gay Concerns of his state psychiatric association. He is the founder and president of a large business and professional organization. At this writing, he and his lover of six years have built their own house and are important activists in the gay community. Both have strong emotional ties to friends, professional associates, and their own and each others' families.

Although I had been a therapist for many years in a practice that included numerous homosexuals, learning about Algy's sexual preference was a humble experience for me. He had grown up with my children, and although I ruminated endlessly about it, I could remember nothing in the long association with this masculine looking, robust, emotionally healthy male that made me suspect he was gay.

Dear Joan had a habit of exaggerating the achievements of those she loved. During one of my last conversations with Algy before his mother died, I said, "I hear you are curing alcoholics. He replied, "I hear you are curing schizophrenics." We both burst out laughing.

One day when Joan and I were to meet for our weekly lunch at the Madison Delicatessen, I waited and waited. Joan never showed up. I called her home and received no answer, so I assumed there had been a misunderstanding about the time or date and ordered my lunch.

That evening Seymour called. Joan had suffered a cerebral hemorrhage, and was in Lenox Hill Hospital.

"I came home from work," he said, "and saw her

lying on the floor at the foot of her closet. At first I thought she was putting on her boots. Then I saw that she was unconscious."

Seymour isn't the kind of man who deceives himself. He knew right away Joan was going to die.

"But she's been a fighter all her life, and she'll fight hard to stay alive," I reassured him (and myself). He wasn't convinced. Joan never recovered consciousness. She was sixty-three years old.

I couldn't believe it. Joan was a happy and fulfilled person, bursting with life, energy, and love for her family and her work. She was one of those pioneer women who truly had it all. No one I know leads a fuller, richer life. But a nagging voice persists, "Your mother died from grief after Zane died. Was there something inside Joan that caused her so much sorrow she couldn't live with it?" Both were grieving mothers. Both died of a cerebral hemorrhage. Was it a coincidence? Despite Joan's wonderful work for gay support, she never stopped mourning her son's "pathology." The bible says, "For of sorrow cometh death, and sorrow of heart will bow down the strength[64]." Such pain never really dissipates, and there comes a time when even one's nearest and dearest can't bear to hear any more about it. Then one is alone with one's grief. Did the anguish of these mothers push so hard for discharge that it rocketed their blood pressure enough to burst a cerebral blood vessel? I know doctors believe a cerebral hemorrhage is caused by a genetic flaw. Nevertheless, something in me will always wonder.

After Joan's death, I dreamed that

Joan gave a party for Frank. There was an admission charge for the "party." I wanted to attend badly, but thought it cost too much.

I awoke thinking, "You're darn right there is a charge to go to the party! The charge is life itself. That's one party I have no plans to attend!"

Then I fell back asleep, and dreamed

Joan and I were sitting in a love seat giggling. I thought, "We'll have to separate those two."

When I awoke again I exclaimed aloud, "That's right! I will not sit with Joan in a love seat or anywhere else,

68

because it is a death seat, not a love seat." I'm glad the dream ended with our having to separate. If I had joined the party, I probably wouldn't be alive today. Like Shakespeare, I say "Live a thousand years, / I shall not find myself so apt to die[65]."

Muhammad[66] said a long time ago, "Death is a bridge that uniteth friend with friend." Not so strange, then, that my dreams after the deaths of my friends led to wishes of joining them, even if it meant dying.

I believe Freud was right. There is a deep death wish buried in each of us. And it is especially strong when those we love have left us.

But do I really want to die? I love my life, I love my family, and I love my friends – those who are left, anyway. I love to write. Why would I possibly want to end it all?

Death is peaceful, a voice within me answers. There are no wars there. There is no racial strife. There are no birth injuries, no mental illness, and no crime. Kennedy said life is not fair, but now he is in a place where all is fair for everyone. Only in death is there equality; then we are all alike. In death, your children and grandchildren are always healthy, happy, and successful. You and your loved ones remain perpetually young and beautiful. You never have the agony of seeing another person you love die. There will be no more rejection slips nor will you have to read the harsh words of a critic. You'll never see your beloved books on a remainder table on sale for twenty-five cents. Or worse, disappear off the face of the earth. You can die believing your next book would have won a Pulitzer Prize. People will think only nice things about you, and forget your traits that made them angry. There will be no hurtful or embarrassing memories, no regrets, no inner pain, no sorrow, no longing, and no loss. You can repose among the trees and flowers forever.

Sounds pretty good to me.... Doesn't everybody feel that way sometimes, if only we would admit it?

So, goodbye, Joan. But know that every time I see a talented young actress, or need a pal to laugh or cry with, or want someone to accompany me to a play or movie on the spur of the moment, or something strikes my funny bone that only you would understand, or I meet parents who have learned to be kind and accepting of their gay or lesbian children, I will think of you and miss you. But most of all, whenever I fall in love with a painting, an opera, a play, or a man, I will long to share the news with you, my simpatico friend. I will all my life.

Part 7: Anna Schwarz

Long before I rebounded from Joan's death, Anna Schwarz was pegged by the Grim Reaper. She and I had sat next to each other in ninth grade home room class at Olney High, and immediately became best friends. I was the first and probably the only close friend she ever had. According to her mother, Anna was an unhappy child until she met me, after which she grew more lighthearted. Her mother said she was perpetually grateful.

Anna was raised in a luxurious suburban home. She was given an exquisite wardrobe, including a sheared beaver coat while she was still in high school. But despite appearances, I believe her early despondency never disappeared but simply went underground. The real love in the Schwarz family seemed to be between the parents, with the children just a sidebar to the main article. The household revolved about Mrs. Schwarz, who was babied and indulged by her husband and children. Anna became an adult long before her time, and learned early on to take care of her mother. "Anna was ready to get married when she was ten years old," Mrs. Schwarz said. All three Schwarz daughters died before their parents. Lovely as the superficialities of

71

their lives were, did the three sisters lack the vital nourishment that enables people to lead long, fulfilled lives?

Was Mrs. Schwarz, despite her outward concern for her children, secretly a selfish and petty woman? An isolated episode suggests that to me. As Anna's best friend, I was often invited to dinner at the Schwarz's. This evening we had finished our meal and were sitting around the kitchen table talking. I remarked that I hated the job I was usually assigned at home of clearing the dishes off the table. Mrs. Schwarz arose and removed everyone else's plate but mine. I felt frozen to my seat and unable to be the only person at the table to move my plate. Today, I would simply get up and take the dish away. But I was only fourteen. Mrs. Schwarz was an adult woman, and should have developed beyond putting a young guest in that position. Fortunately, Anna's sister Helene came to the rescue and graciously took my plate to the sink.

My daughter Janet remembers Anna as a kind and loving person. When asked what she recalls about her, Janet replied, "She was warm, more like an aunt than a friend, nice and funny, with bleached blond hair and a handsome husband. She played golf, wore golf clothes a lot, and did aerobics way back when nobody else did. She seemed like the old fashioned kind of homemaker, whose whole life was devoted to her husband and her children. I remember you told me that her main concern about her daughters was their finding a husband. She said everybody should have a partner. She wanted them to be taken care of as she was. It is sad that Berta didn't marry until after her mother died. It was nice that Anna had two daughters, because we were all girls together. I remember all of us in my room in Beach Haven putting on our bathing suits and laughing."

Anna was a bit plump when we met, but when she was fourteen years old she got the flu and lost a few pounds until she weighed one hundred and ten. She kept that weight all her life, until the end when she wasted away with cancer. As a girl, her hair was her most beautiful feature. It curved off a widow's peak and was the color of wheat fields in the springtime. When she got older she bleached it, and she looked like every other bleached blond. When I told Anna I didn't like the new color, she replied, "Well, that's how it's going to stay the rest of my life!" And it did.

We lived about a mile apart when we were youngsters, and would meet on stone steps at a point midway between our homes. We spent many an afternoon talking and giggling on the steps. Anna was always the first to want to leave. "I have to go home," she would say before the afternoon was over. I couldn't understand why, because there was no one I would rather have been with than Anna. Now I think she was afraid to be away from her mother too long. Years later, I found out she was phobic, and wouldn't go on any trip that would keep her away from home overnight. She returned there to sleep every night, until she and Bert took their first (and last) trip abroad.

When she was fifteen, she got scarlet fever. Her younger sister Helene was her nurse, and the two of them spent all their time in Anna's back room on the third floor. Everyone smoked in those days, but of course Anna was not allowed any cigarettes. I spoke to her on the phone every day, and she rigged up a system whereby she lowered a brown hemp basket down the three stories on a rope. I put cigarettes in the basket, and Anna pulled it up to her room. To my knowledge, the cigarettes didn't prolong her scarlet fever.

I'll never forget when Anna appeared at her window to let down the basket. She looked wizened and yellow, shrunk to half her former size.

Despite her intelligence and insight, when we entered the tenth grade she switched to the Commercial course.

"Why, Anna?" I asked, disconsolate.

"Because I'm going to go to work when I graduate. There is no point in going to college." Years later she asked me, "Why did you let me do it?" As if I could have stopped her!

When Anna died of colon cancer at the age of sixty-three, I went back through my scrapbook to renew old memories. I enjoyed looking at the photos of us playing angels in a Christmas play, the still faintly fragrant dried roses from the senior prom we attended with our dates, the photo of the stiffly posed senior class on our boat trip to West Point, the snapshot of Anna laughing on the boat with her head thrown back in the sunshine, and the graduation program itself, where stars leap out beside both our names for graduation with distinction. Most treasured of all was a letter Anna had written me when she heard about the birth of my son Zane. Anna loved the telephone, and the letter was the only one I ever received from her during our fifty years of friendship. She wrote:

You have a son! I can hardly believe it. I tried to call you, but the hospital said you do not have a phone available to you yet. I'm truly disappointed because no letter could possibly tell you how I feel. I am as happy for you now as I was for me when my Louise was born. All my love goes out to you tonight-and always for happiness and great and wonderful things all your lives.

I especially miss Anna when I am around my children and grandchildren. She would be as happy as I am about Janet's scholarly achievements, Jonny's fantastic success as the president of Kirshenbaum and Bond Advertising Agency, Zane's strength and wisdom, and the happy marriage each has made. But she would be most thrilled about my five beautiful grandchildren. Except for my mother, nobody was as delighted by my children as Anna. She laughed with me about their antics, held them close when they were babies, and empathized with their problems. Once when they were little, one of them had a humiliating accident in Anna's back yard. She hastily clasped the child to her breast, and lovingly reassured the toddler that the world had not come to an end. An infant's hiccups sent Anna into a giggling fit, as if it were the most precious thing in the world. Like the love of a devoted grandmother, her interest and excitement around my children made me enjoy them even more.

When Anna landed a job with an attorney after graduation from high school, she was proud of her salary of ten dollars a week. Her brand new husband was pleased, too, and bragged about it to all his friends. Anna bought a pair of navy blue suede shoes with her first paycheck.

"You just bought a pair of shoes," Bert said.

"Oh Bert," she answered, "Those were sneakers!"

I always assumed the real reason for Anna's change of curriculum was that her mother didn't believe in educating women, since they were only going to get married and have children. I never forgave Anna's parents for that, as they easily could have sent her to the finest of colleges or school of fashion and design. I'm sure Anna's lopped off education is as great a loss to the world as it was to her. A few years before she died, she did go to college, and got a straight A average. But she felt it was too late for a career. She brought up her daughters differently, however. She encouraged Louise to earn a Ph.D. in Russian Literature.

There was another reason Anna didn't go to college earlier, Anna confided to me. She said, "I think I am a little smarter than Bertram, and his college education makes us more equal." Though she returned to school, she never got her diploma. A term before her graduation, Bert decided to take a trip abroad-their first. Anna agreed, and never went back to school. Was Bert's choice of a trip at that time really a coincidence?

Anna was rather vain about her appearance, especially after she married Bertram, a highly successful chiropractor, the kind who has ten patients waiting in ten tiny examining rooms while he darts from one to the other. One day the couple went swimming in a lake a few hours away from their Philadelphia Main Line home. Bert suggested that they meet some friends who lived nearby for dinner. Anna refused. "We should go swimming and out to dinner on different days," she said. After all, her hair was a wreck after she went swimming.

Anna had simple yet elegant taste, of the sort that put the Duchess of Windsor high on the list of the best dressed women of her time. Like the Duchess, Anna could wear a modest sweater and skirt with such style that people turned around to look at her. Of course the sweater and skirt were perfectly cut, with faint apricot and orchid pinks as breathtaking as flowers in a garden. When she was eight months pregnant she came to visit at my parents' home. My mother said, "Anna pregnant looks better than other women not pregnant."

Abounding with talent in many areas, she was a talented dressmaker who designed and sewed her own clothes. I remember a suit the color of bubblegum she made that looked as if it had been fashioned by a couturier. Once when I was visiting her, she lent it to me. I loved wearing it, and have been looking for one like it ever since. A psychoanalyst friend remarked, Anna expresses herself in her clothing. In other aspects of her life, too, such as in her choice of birthday cards. (She never forgot my birthday or the childrens'.) They were all embellished with roses.

When she married at nineteen, she felt a pang of regret that she wasn't joining me at college. "Everybody might think getting married and having children is an ordinary thing," she said wistfully. "But I've never done it before, and it isn't ordinary to me." I thought her words were wise, for a young woman of nineteen. I still do.

When Anna married Bert, something special disappeared from my life. She no longer was there for me in the absolute sense she had been before: She was too busy being Bert's wife. The couple seemed to melt into one another, so that even her body appeared to have a less distinct outline when the two were together. Bert's interests became her interests, his success hers. "We made such and such an amount of money last month," she said. "Our office is being redecorated in wine and pink." She turned into a golfer, a party giver, a Doctor's Wife. She wouldn't even go to the movies in the afternoon with me, if it was a good picture, saying "I have to save that one for Bert."

Anna appeared to be the ideal wife and mother. Her home, with its soft lines and colors and original modern art, was as lovely as her clothing, and she was a devoted homemaker who spent practically all her time and energy caring for her family. She said once in an aside that hurt my feelings, "Children need a full time mother if they are to grow up well." I felt it was a jab at me for having a profession. Perhaps she was jealous of my successful career. I wouldn't be surprised. It may be that growing up in a family where the mother receives the lion's share of love and attention tends to produce envious children. Another time, she categorized her husband's and my professions as second rate doctors. She also chastised me for having a Christmas tree for my children, saying coldly, "They won't know what they are." And even worse, she said, "I wouldn't want my children to live near blacks because when they grow up they might marry one."

In contrast, Anna had an intuitive way of understanding character just by being in someone's presence. When we were seniors in high school, we attended a career conference at Temple University, where a professor spoke on the theatre. Anna said he was a phoney, a conclusion I didn't come to until after I had studied with him for years.

Once we were discussing *King Lear*[67] and the fact that he gave away his kingdom to his daughters, rather than waiting until his death to bequeath his domain to them. "Let that be a lesson to you," Anna said, only half facetiously. "Keep your money!" I can still hear her semi-humorous intonation, "Keep your monn-ey!"

Anna did some lovely things for me that no one else could have done. At my sixtieth birthday party, she brought a photograph album she had especially made up of pictures of us from the time we were romping thirteen-year-olds to matrons approaching old age. Her gift was the hit of the party. The guests spent much of their time looking at the photos tracing Anna's and my evolution from early adolescence to the beginnings of old age. Her generosity had its limitations, however. She didn't make me a copy, and took the album home.

The last time I saw Anna, we were both sixty-three years old. She told me of a fantasy that she had died. "And all the women will come to the *shiva* and bring Bert homemade *kugal*." Her premonition was right on target. She did die, shortly after. I don't know about the *kugal*, but Bert remarried a short while after Anna's death. How prophetic that she pictured herself dying before her cancer even struck! Was the Death Instinct already beckoning from beneath the surface of Anna's psyche? Or was her vision merely the prime example of her intuitive powers?

My friend Kendall was with us, and I didn't feel I could ask Anna the reason she saw herself dying. I will always regret my omission. As my sister says, "We grow too soon old and too late smart."

It is always the telephone, isn't it. This time it was Louise. "My mother died this morning," she said. "She had cancer of the colon and died on the operating table."

The telephone seemed to weigh a ton. I gasped and stuffed my knuckles in my mouth. I hadn't even known Anna was ill. "Why didn't anyone tell me?" I cried. "I would have come to see her."

"She didn't want any visitors," Louise said. "She looked too awful."

Something else I will always regret. There was a small private funeral the next day, held far out in the country in another state, in an area unfamiliar to me. I had no way to get there. "We don't make a fuss about such things in our family," Louise said. "You needn't come." I didn't go.

Anna ostensibly was a happy wife and mother, who lived a full, rich life, filled with art, social activities, golf, a lovely home, and beautiful clothing. But does an unhappy childhood ever completely dissipate? Or did a hidden lack of security deter her from becoming the person she should have been, both as a child and an adult? The suspicion lingers in my mind that Anna, like Shirley, died before her time because she never found out who she was. Despite their success as wives and mothers, both women suffered from lives that were in part unlived.

Confucius had the right idea thousands of years ago when he said that after age fifty we all must find new lives, or we will die. I take this to mean that we come to the end of the road at fifty, and there is no reason to continue the journey if we have already arrived at our destination. We must begin a new voyage, if we are to have a reason to go on living.

A line in *The Magic Mountain*[68] says "...the body triumphs, (when) it wants something different from the soul." Similarly, Robert Burton wrote[69] as far back as 1621, "The body's mischief... proceeds from the soul: and if the mind is not satisfied, the body can never be cured." I believe these women completed the homemaker journey and were unable to find a replacement. Their bodies affirmed their lack of creative fulfillment and could not be cured, although their souls appeared contented enough. If so, we must be grateful to the Feminist Movement, because women no longer have to perish from the anguish of unlived selves.

The memory of a play starring Henry Fonda flashes through my mind. It was so many years ago that I don't remember the name, but the story was about an author who stopped writing because he was convinced he could never become a first rate writer. Shortly after, he developed cancer and died. The play burns in my memory because I believed even then that it contained an eternal truth.

My belief was confirmed when I read a description by Dr. Sam Atkin[70] telling how creativity saved his life. Suffering from Parkinson's Disease, the eighty-nine year old doctor lay in bed utterly exhausted, feeling hopeless, aware that he was sinking fast. "Am I about to sleep forever?" he asked himself. Then, from somewhere a flow of energy arose in him. Atkin wrote, "A burst of ideas floods my brain. I tell myself I must write them down, else they will disappear. I struggle to sit up. It is agony. I drag myself to a half-sitting, half-lying position. I begin to write. I feel ecstatic. I have fought death-at least for the time being. I feel triumphant."

Intrigued, I began a bit of research on the ages of death of various great artists and writers. As a result, I have become further convinced that creativity is an important factor in keeping people alive. George Bernard Shaw produced some of his most brilliant plays is his sixties and seventies, and wrote until he died at age ninety-four. Sophocles wrote *Oedipus at Colonus* at the age of ninety, shortly before his death. Pablo Casals emerged from retirement when he was seventy-five to play the cello and direct at the Prades Music Festivals in Southern France, and died at the age of ninety-seven. Pablo Picasso continued to produce some of his best works until he died at ninety-one. Martha Graham gave her last dance performance when she was seventy-six years old and continued directing and choreographing until she died at ninety-seven. Marc Chagall attained the age of ninety-six, Frank Lloyd Wright ninety, and Georgia O'Keeffe lived to be one hundred.

An article on Charlotte Perriand[71], a furniture

designer who worked in Corbusier's shadow, reflects on her work from the vantage point of ninety-three years. She is convinced that her personal philosophy is responsible for longevity. In every important decision, she says, there is one option that represents life, and that is what you must choose. Anything else is regressive and, in the philosophy of Freud, a surrender to the Death Instinct. Such acts as preparing for a retrospective exhibition, giving an interview, or writing her memoirs require Perriand to revisit the past and interrupt the progressive flow of her creativity..."Life," she says, "is something in motion." I believe along with Perriand that if Shirley and Anna had chosen the option of life over the conventional pattern for wives and mothers, they would still be alive today.

A review of a concert by the aged violinist, Sephane Grappeli, suggests that he has a similar philosophy of creativity and life. According to the review, he has retained all his talent, skill, and endurance into his extremely advanced years. The reviewer, Matt Ruhdell[72], states:

Admiration isn't the word for it, and neither is respect. What Sephane Grappeli inspired in his audience Wednesday at the Duncan Theatre in Lake Worth was more akin to awe, reverence and love.

He is 88 years old and now performs from a wheelchair, but the great French violinist proved that his refined abilities have not faded with age...

...there was nothing frail or out of date about Grappelli's performance. You would think no one could make any fresh musical comments on Cole Porter's *I Get a Kick Out of You*, yet Grappelli opened with an abstract, almost atonal introduction that dressed the tune in a new, vibrant style.....

All evening long, Grappelli played in perfect time and pitch, soared through operatic cadenzas and sewed his solos together without a seam.

The appreciative audience gave him four standing ovations. He deserved all of that, and more.

Another kind of creativity was demonstrated by an elderly doctor, the paramour of a patient of mine. A few years before I left my practice, a woman in her late eighties consulted me about a sexual problem. It seemed her lover of ninety-two years was sexually insatiable. He still wanted sex at least three times a night and was disturbing her sleep. When asked for my advice, I said some women would consider her lucky. She resolved her problem by permitting him his pleasures, but asking him to allow her to experience fewer orgasms of her own.

My omnipresent fantasy is to join the ranks (with the possible exception of the satyr doctor) of these great artists. But pursuing such an ambition is dangerous, as well as life enhancing. I dread to think of what would happen to me if I were permanently unable to write. That is one reason I'm upset when I can't even scribble in my journal. A comic strip in the *Key West Citizen*[73] speaks of my worst fears, "I've given up hoping that my dreams would come true. Now I just hope that my nightmares don't!"

The caption isn't funny; it is too true to be good. John Barrymore said it better, "A man is really old when regrets take the place of dreams." Yes, I thought, and that is when a person dies.

Thinking of John Barrymore reminds me of one of my favorite jokes[74]. Barrymore has gone to a funeral, where he sees an old man standing at the graveside. Barrymore quips, "It hardly pays to go home!"

I like this one, too. An inscription on a wall in Bermondsey Antique Market said:
"John Wayne is dead."
Underneath in another, more ghostly hand,
"The Hell I am!"[75]

I return to thoughts of Anna. She had talents she used only sporadically, and I bitterly regret she never was able to find one meaningful enough to keep her alive. I wish she had gone to F.I.T. and become a dress designer. As her closest friend, I believe it would have kept her alive.

She gave a lot to me, and asked very little in return. I wish she had asked more. In one of my dreams,
I am standing outside of my house with Brenda, an obese friend who has recently suffered a heart attack. Her skin is the color of sand when the tide runs out, and she looks as if she could die at any moment. Anna is standing in the front

of a brightly lit hall. The light is strong, as if coming through a tunnel. It reminds me of a near-death experience I had after my devastating car accident, in which I envisioned the light at the end of a tunnel. I ask Anna to take care of Brenda, who I feel stands for my aging self. Although Anna turns away, I am certain that when the time comes, she will do as I ask.

Although we were the same age, Anna had been slightly ahead of me in a number of respects, and helped me through many of the exigencies of adolescence. She served as a role model when I didn't know what to wear, how to behave, which fork to use. Once I considered going into the Miss America contest, and acting a scene from a play as my entry in the talent show. Anna said she thought it would cheapen me to enter the contest. I listened to her, and didn't apply. In retrospect, it was no great loss. I'm sure I wouldn't have won anyway. Nevertheless, I wonder why she discouraged me, and wish I had tried.

Anna, in the role of good mother, advised me about the parameters of necking. She didn't know what was right for herself either, but somehow when she told me what she allowed, it gave me permission to do without guilt what I was already doing. Later I admired her example of a young wife living harmoniously with a husband she loved.

And now, with a pain in my chest sharp as a knife cut, I realize she has preceded me again. I am calling her in the dream to help me navigate uncharted waters once more, to teach me how to grow old and die.

An urge to write about Anna has been with me for a long time. When she married at nineteen, I began writing a description of her wedding, which I wanted to be a loving and precious memento to Anna for the rest of her life. But somehow, the article never got off the ground. It was a nice thought, but I was not into weddings at that time. My most notable memory about it is that my gold slippers hurt too much for me to enjoy dancing with my partner. It would be almost eight years before I married Rudy, when I was able to appreciate the elaborate details and extensive planning required for a wedding as lovely as Anna's. Instead of writing it up, my gift to the new couple was a pair of silver frames for their wedding photos.

This memoir is my recompense to you, Anna, for failing to follow through on your wedding.

Remembering their wedding brings the realization that Bert was the third available widower left behind by a close friend of mine. I ask myself if I should contact him, to find out whether we possibly could become an "item." Previous experience again tells me it wouldn't work. I had dated Bertram before Anna. We had double dated, Bertram and I, and Anna with a psychologist named Harvey. During the evening, Bert and Harvey decided they preferred each other's dates to the ones they were with, and switched girls. The men were right by fifty percent; Anna and Bert remained together until her death.

I am sure that what didn't work for me fifty years ago won't work any better today. As I briefly wondered if Bert and I could have an intimate relationship, I reacted much as I had to the thought of marrying Joan's husband, Seymour Smith, and Jill's husband, Barry Barton. I was right all three times. My intuition has remained true. Anyway, I doubt if there is a single man in the world who could replace Rudy.

I awoke this morning with the phrase <u>I miss you. Come back to me</u> on my mind. To whom was the dream referring? I don't know. I miss them all.

Oh friendship, friendship, deep wine colored, velvety friendship, come back to me now from thy watery grave of a million frozen tears.

Anna's daughter Louise recently said to me, "People say the pain of loss gets better as time passes. It doesn't. It gets worse." Freud, in a little known letter to Samuel Freud[76] written after the deaths of his daughter and grandson, agrees with Louise. He writes:

Although we know that after such a loss the acute stage of mourning will subside, we also know we shall remain inconsolable and will never find a substitute....it is the only way of perpetuating that love we do not want to relinquish.

That is my experience, too, Louise. The deaths of mother, father, brother, husband, and friends have ripped holes in the fabric of my existence that no seamstress can repair.

Oh Anna, my Anna, beacon of my teenage years, I don't know how to grow old. I don't know how to live with the terror of evaporating into nothingness. I don't know how to live with the petty tyrannies of a disintegrating body. I don't know how to live with the pain of losing those I love. You were always there to help me navigate the whirling tides of life. Where are you now when I need you to guide me through the shards of old age?

Part 8: Jill Bronson

October 14

Jill Bronson was my next friend to go.

She was twenty-five and I a young seventeen when we met. Jill was a small feisty blond woman whose eyes were keen chips of blue that looked deep into your heart and soul. She greeted me sharply, as if her mouth were a pair of scissors slashing down on each word. I didn't like her much; I thought she was kind of nervy. We spent the summer acting at the Straight Wharf Theatre on Nantucket Island, Massachusetts, an old stock company which smelled of the sea and centuries of musty rope which had been warehoused there.

As roommates in a nine by twelve box in the home of the Xerxa's, a couple connected with the theatre, we mainly tried to keep out of each other's hair. The theatre was rehearsing "Little Women," Jill playing Amy and I, Beth. All of a sudden, it seemed, I chanced on the right way to study a part, until I realized that Jill had quietly been teaching me how to act. I had not acted professionally before, and it was the first time I had ever been away from home. I wonder if I could have made it without Jill, who became my teacher, mentor, and surrogate mother. I loved her a lot.

The quality of love an adolescent girl feels for her mentor is extremely intense. In later years I was to love my husband, adore my children, and worship my grandchildren. But the time Jill and I spent together was a time apart, a dream come true for an aspiring young actress.

One day, after I had been criticized by the director Margaret Fawcett Wilson for my reading of some line or other, I lay crying on my little iron bed. Jill came over and silently stroked my forehead. After that, I cherished her. I had been an isolated child, who rarely touched or was touched by anyone. Jill taught me not to be afraid to show affection. She enabled me to love my husband and children. The entire family owes her an eternal gift of gratitude.

Now there was no acting on our part in the play: we were Beth and Amy, two sisters who adored one another. I loved Jill with a love that was to last until she died of Alzheimer's Disease fifty-three years later.

Little Women was the theme of the summer. On opening night, Jill sent me a box of graceful rosebuds nestling in silver sprays. A note in it said, "Be good, Beth dear-a little for the audience, and a little for me, but mostly for yourself." I was carried away with happiness when Jill said after opening night, "Little Almar is an actress at last! I'm proud of you." The comments in the theatre guest book, "Beth and Amy best ones in show," and "Beth the Camille of the coming generation," bore out her comments, as did the review of the town newspaper which spoke of "Beth's restrained, simple, sincere, beautiful acting." So I was shocked when the director, who never really liked me, decided the play ran too long, and cut down the scene in which Beth dies. It was my favorite scene, and I died with great pleasure every night. I must have been in love with death. I guess somewhere deep down I still am, and that is what this memoir is all about.

After the rehearsal, I rushed down to the Children's Beach and ran along the ocean front sobbing. Suddenly on that clean beautiful night I saw Jill walking against the wind, profiled against the sky. She knew exactly where to find me. I was filled with a wild mixture of joy and sadness, as we strolled the beaches together, Jill's face veering to the mountains, mine to the sea. That night I went to sleep seeing moving pictures in my head of Jill and Nantucket-so close I could almost touch the town clock.

One night when Jill couldn't sleep she woke me at three in the morning to go swimming under the stars. We swam side by side through the clear cold water until we reached a raft and climbed up on it. With choked sobs, Jill revealed the unsavory details of her aborted love affair. I listened silently, as she shared her anguish. Then she asked me to promise never to divulge the tragedy of her life. I never have...

Before we dove off the raft, Jill put her hand on my shoulder. Then I knew the relationship wasn't one-sided and Jill needed me too.

We liked to walk in the rain together. I enjoyed the torrents of summer rain pouring down from the skies until my head was covered with medusa-like snakes. Jill particularly loved to walk in the rain in the dark, and said, "The slick, slick night is shiny as patent leather shoes." The poet and artist in her loved to see the light distorted in the flat, wet depths of the streets.

Jill was called home when her father became ill, neither of us knowing if she could come back or if we would ever see each other again. We silently walked to the wharf, where the boat was to take her to the train on the mainland. She hugged me goodbye, saying, "Who ever thought it would be like this?" I watched her waving on the boat until it disappeared into the horizon. Later she said, "When the boat left everyone grew smaller and smaller, and you were the last one to leave." As I watched, the heavy fog (pronounced fawg) rolled in, as the fog horn mournfully wailed its good-byes. Seven long days later found me waiting by the shimmering sparkling ocean for Jill to return home.

The day before we left Nantucket, Jill gave me a picture of herself. Her face smiled out over the inscription, "In memory of a smile, a sigh, and a tear!" The night we took our last walk on Jetties Beach, we walked in reverential silence, as the pounding surf and rippling harbor joined in harmony. A celestial orchestra of the sea, the harbor, crickets, the wind, and the night seemed to play, "Calm as the night, deep as the sea, my love for thee must be." Then Jill's voice rang out across the water, as she sang "Sylvia's hair is like the night," a song I would always love. After tracing the pattern of the silvery moonbeams in the water, I tried to memorize the cliffs, the sea, the sky, and Jill's face.

"Jill, I'm scared. I'm afraid things won't be the same for us after we leave Nantucket," I said, as we sat on our little iron beds. Jill took my hand in hers and said, "How could we ever forget one another, Almar? If we were miles apart for years and years I'm sure we only would have to think of each other to know things will always be the same between us."

The day we left, someone wrote in the *Boston Post*, "If we could know how and when we shall meet our friends again, our parting would be tenderer." Jill and I read it together on the boat to Woods Hole, and wept. Then we leaned over the railing, trying to catch the shimmering, sparkling water. Jill went off to her poetry, her painting, her acting, and her day job in the book department of Fox's Department Store in Farmington, Connecticut, and I enrolled as a freshman at Temple University in Philadelphia.

The summer had a deep effect on the creativity of us both. Jill's paintings for years reflected the stark beauty of the Nantucket beaches, the crashing waves and sunlight harbor framed by the peaceful mountains she loved. My writing, too, was fueled by loving memories of Jill. A story I wrote for Freshman English Composition (which, incidentally, provided much of the material for this chapter) was called *A Diary of Memories*. My professor, Miss Charlotte, returned it with the comment, "A relationship of psychic homosexuality." I was horrified, but in later years thought Ms. Charlotte was probably correct.

Jill was an unusual artist, distinguished by her sensitive talent as well as a lack of interest in selling her work. Although it was of professional caliber and greatly admired by other artists, she had no desire to show it. She refused to spend her precious time contacting galleries, and even turned down a few who sought her out. In a sense she was a true artist, painting for her own pleasure and not for money. She followed her inner standards and not what was au courant in the art world. I cradle a secret hope that Jill's genius will be discovered posthumously and that some day she will receive the acclaim she deserves.

I will always treasure a painting Jill did of me in Nantucket. She had caught me in a reflective black mood, locked into some long forgotten misery. It was a self that was familiar to me, an Almar, although not many others recognized it as Alma. Before beginning the painting Jill asked, "What could be so awful as to bring on that look?" No one else had ever seen so deeply into my soul.

Jill was a person guided by her own needs and not what others thought. Once during a visit with me, she had a miserable cold which left her with an inflamed nose. To remedy this she swabbed it with Vaseline. Jill's nose was unusually long, and the smeared Vaseline did not add to her beauty. Anna and Bert were coming to meet Jill for the first time. I hinted to her that she would look more attractive if she removed the grease from her nose.

"They'll just have to like me this way, dear," Jill answered.

Years later when our families were spending the summer at Beach Haven, New Jersey, I invited Jill over to visit with some mutual friends who had expressed a desire to see her. She said it wasn't worth it to leave her painting to be with them, even if they would be insulted. She already realized at age forty that an artist's life is short, and there is never enough time to complete one's work.

"August is gone, before I've turned around," she said poetically. "And all the dandelions have blown away in cloudy smoke." Another time she said, "We live too fast-There is no song to catch the sudden white tenderness of blossoms."

We continued our friendship with visits, letters, and phone calls. Jill further entwined herself in my life by making her Philadelphia friends my friends, which greatly enhanced the pleasure of my college days. She had two other young friends at Temple who adored her, Marion and Cally. We sort of formed a Jill Bronson Fan Club, which helped Jill's and my friendship to stay sparkling and alive.

The influence we had on each other determined even the men we married. I had gone out first with Barry Barton, and told him I thought he would prefer my friend Jill. I was right. He went to see her in a play, fell in love, and turned out to be the ideal husband for her.

She was a wonderfully involved mother, who enjoyed and adored her children, and was always dreaming up creative ways to stimulate their interest in intellectual and creative ideas. Jill and Barry frequently took their offspring to Broadway plays and concerts. Jill said she considered it part of their education. The family invented several make-believe characters who paid recurrent visits to the dining room table. Jill's persona was the Spanish lady. Barry's was Shnoonie, two fingers that traipsed back and forth across the table and spoke to everybody. The resourceful atmosphere paid off in developing the children's creativity. Daniel is now a photojournalist for a prominent radio station and Tracy, the editor-in-chief of an erudite magazine, is the author of two scholarly books.

I decided to ask Tracy if she would E-Mail me memories of her mother. Surprisingly to me, who had known the family from it's beginning, Tracy's response cast a somewhat different light on the patterns within it. But then, who ever really knows what goes on behind closed doors?

"Dear Alma:" she wrote,
"You ask what sort of mother Jill was. She was an archetypal force filling heaven and earth.
Her love was fierce, relentless, inescapable.
"Her life was underscored by a great longing for wonder and magic. As a young woman she had been nearly alone in her faith-devastatingly alone. But she was able to raise her children in it.
"She did it by means of her imagination, in which she was happy as a silver fish. What fun we had--the fairy tales, the painting expeditions, the rocks, the shells, the bird sightings, the stories by our bedside at night. How many people she turned into, and how many delicious secret places we found!
"From infancy on, I felt myself the instrument of my mother's desire. She was a passionate person, and she focused all her joy, celebration, and gratitude upon me. I

90

was wonderful. I was destined for greatness. I was her fairy child. One does not have to advance far into infancy, however, before continuous wonderfulness gets to be a heavy load.

"It was not possible for me to reach her objective by following the path she took. And yet she had her wish. The daughter realized the mother's dreams-but not in the forms she'd had in mind. She passed into old age without ever recognizing that her goal was won.

"There were realms in which we never met. Most mothers instruct their daughters in being female. We had no sharing there. I had to pass through that labyrinth alone.

"Mom and Dad were both emotional, both vulnerable in unexpected ways, and both a little given to theatrics. They came from different backgrounds and had different expectations of domestic order. The clouds would gather and the storms would break, and all of it was just the business of their relationship. All of which gives the impression that the tone of our household was unbrokenly melodramatic, but it wasn't really. The family glue was warmth, which tied together all members. There was plenty of expressed physical affection; I relied upon it heavily (and still do).

"I decided that all my family members were subject to fits of temporary insanity, so I was going to explain them all to one another and single-handedly make the family work to my satisfaction.

"The results were that I was tired and depressed most of the time, and that I moved nearly all of my own life out of the human arena and into the world of books. So things stayed well into high school, until everything came apart when I ran away to Los Angeles.

"The story of LA is the story of Persephone. Nobody ever asks whether it would have been good for the girl to be the darling mirror of Demeter indefinitely, or whether, considering the seamlessness and depth of the love that bound them, there could have been any workable escape from it other than some form of abduction. Nor does anybody ask whether Persephone might not have felt herself embracing destiny when she ate those pomegranate seeds.

"One of the most important things I got from my year

in therapy was a classic piece of psychoanalytic material: just how much I loved my father. There was a moment when I was two years old when that love exploded in me: he was suddenly the most beautiful creature conceivable. But to love my father was to trespass in my mother's private domain. And so I gave him up. That same year I read my first word.

"Not surprisingly, when adolescence hit I found I was quite comfortable with men intellectually, but terrified of them sexually.

"So how many options had Persephone?"

The Bartons were unusually creative in many aspects of their lives. My daughter Janet especially remembers their brilliant Christmas cards. Photos of the family were pasted over hand drawn characters in current or political events. Historical milestones such as the landing of man on the moon were peopled with photos of the Bartons. Once they were Santa and Mrs. Claus, pulling their children and a sleighful of toys in the sky. The collection of cards is a veritable record of the history of four decades. Some enterprising company could make a fortune publishing them.

Jill, like Anna, was as industrious a dressmaker as she was in other areas of her life, and sewed many of her own clothes to perfection. In fact, when a study[77] came out suggesting a link between Alzheimer's Disease and people who were exposed to electromagnetic radiation, like seamstresses who spent a lot of time nose to nose with their sewing machines, I wondered if Jill's exacting work had inadvertently led to her death. Her designs were typical Lord and Taylor, meticulously sewn, so that one could not tell her hand made stitches from those done by machine. She was the most fastidious person I had ever known, in her sewing and in her life, and was not above scrubbing her kitchen floor at two A.M.

"If it needs to be done, I'm going to do it," she exclaimed.

I once had a dream in which a voice said, *Jill's wheels have no grease.*

Barry's warmth and love provided the soil for the flowering of Jill's womanhood, and helped her develop from

92

a repressed WASP to a sensual, warm wife, mother, artist, and poet. When Barry heard I was writing about Jill, he sent me a letter he'd found tucked in the back of her bureau drawer as he was cleaning it out. It had been written fifteen years earlier, to the day. He said he was "enclosing a copy rather shamefacedly, because it might affect your depiction of her as wife and mother." It didn't, because I already knew what a devoted husband he was, and how much Jill had appreciated him.

Darling Barry (it said):

Author of all good things. This non card is to say I love you; and to wish you all joy and good things this earth has to offer you.

Thank you for the good life you have given me-a beautiful home, two fine and intelligent children (they take after you) and much fun and adventure and variety and surprise.

May the good Lord Bless and keep you.
Much love,
Your thirty year wife,
Jill

I wonder how many wives could write such sentiments to their husbands thirty years after the wedding.

A poem Jill wrote about growing old together further documents her ever expanding growth and love...

Love Then, Love Now
I can remember when
Your cheek was seamless,
Smooth as unsewn silk,
Your hair berry black,
Crisp as grasses in the snow,
And your kisses fell
like red blossoms
On my pale breast.

Now your cheek is creased
From passing years,
Your black hair
A thin winter snow,

Yet your kisses,
Red blossoms in the night,
Still fall with passion
On my pale breast.

...until she reached another stage, where even Barry's love
was only of limited protection:

Being Old
I know
What it is like to be old.
It is to carry the weight of the bones
The length of a tired day,
To feel pain like a gray mouse
Nibbling life away.
It is the winding of each day
Upon a spool.
Colorless is the wool on the spool.
And the heavy nights come down
And close in...
And these are wound
On spools of pain,
And thin is the wool on the spool.
This is being old--
One more day,
Another night,
Stored away.

During the last horrible years of her life, Barry
nursed her, fed her spoonful by spoonful, and dressed her,
always speaking in a kind, loving manner. Shortly before she
died, I asked him, "Don't you ever get angry with Jill? She
doesn't listen to you, and often is uncooperative about
getting dressed, eating, etc. etc." He answered, "I sometimes
get angry with the illness, but never with her." At the end, if
he weren't with her she would clamp her lips together like a
recalcitrant baby and refuse to eat.

On one of her more lucid days after she was
diagnosed with Alzheimer's, I asked her, "How is it for you,
living with such a terrible illness?" She answered, "It is
worse for the others than it is for me."

I knew I had influenced Jill in many areas of her life, but the best thing I ever did for her was introduce her to Barry Barton.

Barry was so splendid a husband that after Jill died I invited him to come to Key West and visit me, partly to grieve together, and partly to see if we could share our lives. But although I consider him a dear friend, I can't picture us in a more intimate relationship. He is small and dark, and Rudy's strong, teddy bear look still haunts me. Also, when I reflect on it, I realize I was thinking of Barry as an old man. What do I want with an old man in his seventies? I mused. Then I thought, Wait a minute! *I'm* in my seventies....

What's wrong with me? Here are three superior husbands of three dear friends, and I don't want any of them! As I had done with Anna's husband, Bert, I had dated Barry before his wife did, and hadn't seen him as a potential husband even then. With me, such feelings last. It is a truism that anyone who didn't attract me when I was young won't now, either.

The influence Jill and I had on each other was mutual. When I first considered marrying Rudy Bond, I had some question about it. My parents thought the eleven year difference in our ages was too great, and disapproved of his profession. They were European immigrants, and according to them, in Europe an actor is only a little better than a bum. I told Jill about their objections, showed her his picture (which was inscribed "I'll always love you") and asked what she thought.

"Look how you are running your hand over his lips," she replied. "That should answer your question!" Then she added, "He makes the boys you go out with look like callow youths." She later told me she thought it was a good match because he brought me down to earth. I accepted Rudy's proposal. We stayed married until he died almost forty years later.

As with many of us, perhaps all was not as it seemed in Jill's life. That she was ready to die even before she became ill is sadly evident in one of her last poems:

Death
Long have I loved death
And known his presence.
Comfortable dark friend,
I hold his hand
Across a thousand miles of light,
My true partner in the dance.

Why should a woman who seemed so fulfilled in marriage, motherhood, creativity, and career be in love with death? Why should she consider death to be her "true partner"? Is it possible that in a place deep inside herself she never really found what she wanted?

After one of Jill's visits, I found a poem she had left for me on a scrap of paper:

Wail
The earth I hate
And all things on it!
Each animal and man,
My weakly whitely body-
Shun it!
Damn the Eternal Plan!

No, despite Jill's seemingly full life, something fundamental and indispensable was missing in her. A memory flashed through my mind of the time a friend of Jill's had become openly homosexual.

"How disgusting!" Jill's mother said. "They should be arrested. They'll give each other all kinds of diseases."

Jill's domineering, cold mother was no more understanding of her daughter's needs than those of her lesbian friend's. Jill yearned for something-she knew not what-all her life. Her mother had been the dominant parent, and Jill's traveling-salesman father seemed little more than an appendage of the all-powerful mother. The family had to struggle for money to live on. After high school Jill sold books for four years in Wanamaker's Department Store to save enough money to go to college. She had been a deprived child and a deprived adolescent, and despite her loving and beloved family in adulthood and her flourishing creativity, I don't believe she ever got over her early deprivation. She remained "hungry" all her life, as illustrated in the following poem:

Rebirth
I walked me to my place of eating
but have not eaten-
I fed on bits of cloud
that passed me by...

It was not my stomach
that was hungry-
it was I...

I learned in my practice that people who feel unloved as babies are likely to have a strong death wish. Perhaps even as an infant, Jill longed for the quiet comfort of the grave, the closest she could come to the lost intrauterine paradise. Now, after eighty years of yearning, she finally met her true partner in the dance.

Jill understood how much it hurts to feel unloved. Once after she died, when I was feeling rotten and rejected by the world, I felt a delicate hand upon the top of my head.

"Who are you?" I murmured.

"Jill," came a whisper soft as a summer mist. "Have you forgotten I love you? I told you in Nantucket that if we were miles apart for years and years we have only to think of each other to know things will always be the same between us. Remember it, Almar. We meant too much to each other for you to toss it away."

Of course, I thought, the feel of that hand can only be Jill's, expressing boundless love through her sensitive artist's fingers. No one else had so tender and affectionate a touch.

Was it really Jill come to visit? The answer doesn't matter. I felt better anyway. In fact I felt wonderful.

Part 9: New Friends, Old Friends, and the Depleted Quotidian

November 13

Disaster drains the human spirit, and I had no energy to look for new friends to replace those I'd lost. Then one night, after months, even years of grieving,

I dreamed of an old rotary phone which had colored circles pasted on it. Printed on the circles were phone numbers. In the dream I crossed out the old numbers and replaced them with new ones. I woke up feeling marvelous, as if I had accomplished something momentous.

A few days later, I walked into my friend Elizabeth's house, where I had been invited for dinner. All of a sudden three people leaped out at me and yelled, "Surprise!" I had forgotten it was my birthday. My friends had prepared all my favorite foods, including deserts, as delicious as lo-fat and lo-calorie food can be, even to the birthday cake with candles saying seventy (ugh!) on the cake. Lois, another good Key West friend who was out of town, sent a lovely bouquet of roses. The birthday presents were exactly what I would have chosen for myself, a great book by Anita Brookner from June, a pair of shell earrings from Maria, and the following card from Elizabeth:

Birthday Celebration
for
Alma H. Bond, Ph.D.
Dinner at the Key West Cafe of Your Choice
Possibilities include but are not limited to:
Cafe des Artistes
Nina's Cafe Cay Creole
Cafe Alia
Banana Cafe
Cafe Marquesa
or Cafe Sole

These are my favorite restaurants in Key West. If Elizabeth missed one, I can't think of it. It was the first birthday since Shirley's death that I enjoyed.

When I came home, I found birthday messages from seven other friends on my answering machine. The dream of the rotary phone was certainly prescient!

I told my daughter-in-law Wendy about the party and the messages and said, "And I'm always complaining that I don't make close friends any more!" Wise Wendy said, "I think your Key West friends are closer than you know!"

Speaking of Elizabeth, whoever would think that ideas on aging and death could make people laugh? But that's what happened last night, when my brilliant forty-year old friend and I got together for dinner at Boston Chicken Market. Elizabeth decided my journal had to be published, and enthusiastically began marketing plans for a book to be based on it and entitled, *Old Age is a Terminal Illness*. I wrote what she said on a paper napkin.

"The cover should have a black lace border around it. And the book can be packaged in a box like a tiny casket, which opens up like a coffin, lined of course in black. You will need to give a mourning book party in which no one will be admitted who isn't wearing black. Market the book in funeral parlors as well as regular bookstores. Do you know how many funeral parlors there are, Alma? Some are even franchised! Imagine the kind of distribution you'd get if you connect with one of those. A free copy with every funeral! And you must have alternate titles for the book, with a different one like 'Death' for the funeral parlors, because mourners will not appreciate the humor in *Old Age is a Terminal Illness*. Insurance companies could include a free copy with renewals of life insurance. Sales would go so fast in hospital gift shops and retirement homes they wouldn't be able to keep the book in stock. And think of how many copies would sell on Halloween!"

Then Eileen Walkenstein, my psychiatrist friend, came to visit, for the first time in years. We had gone to grammar school together. I was relieved that at least one of my contemporaries was still around. Eileen read a poem she had written. It exactly expressed the way I feel:

Me – and the Tree
Where have all your leaves gone?
To the ground,
To the ground.

Where is all the rustling?
Not a sound,
Not a sound.

Where are all your colors?
Fade away,
Fade away.

Why does all this happen?
End of day,
End of day.

Will you bloom again then?
In the Spring,
In the Spring.

And your colors bring then?
I will bring,
I will bring.

My eyes and ears are dimming
Fade away,
Fade away.

Why does all this happen?
End of day.
End of day.

When she finished reading her poem, I blinked away a tear. I was not surprised that Eileen had written it, for she is a woman like Kendall Kane who faces her feelings, no matter how painful. She is in excellent shape, both emotionally and physically. Part of her mental health regime is to express her angry feelings whenever she can. I was envious when we went out to dinner together, and Eileen repeatedly asked the waiter for what she wanted. She didn't hesitate to say, "More onions, please...May I have more sauce for the spaghetti? It's a little dry...More water, please, with a little lemon in it." The waiter obliged with a pleasant demeanor, and didn't seem to mind at all.

"Don't you care if he is annoyed with you?" I asked.

"Of course I care. We have to live with people. But we are paying for service, and I have to speak up for what I need."

Eileen also has a wonderful physical health agenda. She carefully monitors what she eats, and rarely puts a spoonful of fat or sugar into her mouth. She drinks no coffee, tea, or liquor. Instead, every morning she swallows a gallon (!) of water, as she believes it washes the toxicity out of her body. She walks everywhere, at least four miles a day. Then she spends several hours at a gym lifting weights. No wonder she has the lean body of a well-exercised adolescent! At an age when many of my contemporaries (the ones who are still alive) move about with a walker, have had heart surgery or cancer, or are crippled with arthritis, I find it hard to believe this vigorous creature is over seventy years old. It's true that Eileen's face up close is rather wrinkled, like the creases in rumpled, smoothed out Kleenexes. But I'm happy to find someone who has preserved at least as much health and energy as I. "See," I tell myself, "you don't have to become a basket case when you get old!"

I found myself smiling as I recalled Eileen as a child of eight. She had a round pleasant face, rosy cheeks, a perpetual smile which displayed two rows of broad white teeth, eyes like two black glass globes, and thick raven pigtails down to her shoulders. She looked like a farmer's innocent child. In fact, she had kept her innocence for a long time. She was the only girl I knew who bragged that she was sweet sixteen and never been kissed. Now the broad smile beams through the wrinkled seventy-year-old face.

These days I read the obituaries daily. Last week all of a sudden my own face leaped out at me. I bent over the paper and examined the portrait closely, and of course, it wasn't me. The dead woman didn't even resemble me. But what does the delusion say about my state of mind, that I unconsciously expect to be in the obituaries at any moment? Not if my conscious mind has any say in the matter! I reread the list of the newly departed, and was a little comforted to see that many were in their eighties and older. But not all. An awful lot were in their seventies. To my surprise, I found myself thinking about reincarnation after death. Perhaps the thought was inspired by Eileen's poetic verse:

Will you bloom again then?
In the Spring,
In the Spring.

Far Eastern religions teach that living beings have many lives, with goodness rewarded by rebirth in a more advanced form. Reincarnation is an ethical philosophy in which good is rewarded and evil punished. If there is a God, He has to be a bleeding heart liberal who understands why we are the way we are and do the evil we do, and is far above petty judgments. As Heine said on his deathbed, "God will pardon me. It's his métier[78]." The idea of reincarnation has never made any sense to me. I think the party will go on, but I won't be invited. Although I must admit rebirth sounds a bit more plausible when one is reading daily obituaries. I cannot believe in the doctrine because nature is vastly indifferent to our individual fates, and could care less about human ideals of right and wrong. They change with the times, anyway. Thinking the earth moves around the sun almost got Galileo killed by the Inquisition only a few centuries ago. His belief was considered sacrilegious. Neither hurricanes nor scorpions recognize virtue. It rains upon the just as well as the unjust. The good die right along with the bad. The life of a person, be s/he good or evil, is of no more concern to the universe than the life of an ant. I decided this when I was eight years old, as I was knocked down by a huge wave and dragged down under the water. As I desperately floundered about and swallowed a quart of water, I thought, "The ocean doesn't care if I live or die." I believe along with the new science that if we exist at all after death, it will be at the level of the neutrino, in an as-yet-unimaginable dimension of space and time.

So after finding my face in the obituary column, I was startled to find myself wondering what manner of creature I would choose to be reborn as, in the highly unlikely probability that I were given a choice." Me!" I thought, without missing a beat. "I want to be reborn as me." I chuckled as I was reminded of Camus's condemned criminal in *The Stranger*, who, on being asked how he pictured the afterlife, answered, "One where I could remember this life!"

What is the value of a life, anyway? To what extremes should we go to preserve one? I saw a TV program in which a whale had gotten its tail jumbled up in a lobster net and wasn't able to untangle itself. The creature was frantic and kept thrashing about in the water until it began to bleed. The whale was sighted by the Coast Guard, who went to great lengths to rescue the creature, even to risking the life of a scientist. Coming close enough to look down into the eyes of the whale, he was able to sever the bonds that imprisoned it. As soon as it was freed, the whale swam off into the deep.

I idly wondered why people don't go to the same extremes to extend, for example, the life of an ant. Isn't it possible somewhere in the Great Scheme of Things its value is as significant as ours? I am not against the saving of whales, nor do I harbor any particular affection for insects. I am only questioning whether we measure the value of a life by size. Albert Schweitzer didn't. He literally never killed a fly, but would open the door and shoo the insect outside. Is this an example of his greatness of heart that we can't afford outside of the jungle? I would like to emulate him, but would consider it a bit discombobulating to live in a house full of

104

mice and roaches.

The mother of my close friend of many years, Dr. Arlene Richards, died a few weeks ago. Arlene and I share interests in psychoanalysis, writing, our children, and each other. She is a rare woman of many talents; therapist, writer, mother, wife, activist, humanitarian, and is one of those people who enriches the lives of those about them. Arlene has tamed her grief by writing poetry. I just received the following poem from her:

Mother's Night
Less days
less height.
Less.
As she dies, my mother grows less.
Even her skin grows tight.
Less.
Her lids droop.
Her gaze is less.
Her hands grasp air.
Her smile loses curvature.
A moon no longer cup, now saucer.
STOP TIME.
Go no further.
Because I, the one to bring home blue stars
need you to bring them home to.
And him.
The one you meant to be baby
and cuddle and
take.
How will he live without
the thirst he brings you?

Who is he, who am I
When you have no lap for us
to bring them to?

Arlene, I weep for you, and for all of us motherless orphans.

My friend Rosa told me a strange story. Joe, a bar tender in Key West, had a crush on Rosa, and frequently spoke of her to the owner of the bar where he worked. It seems Joe, who had no family, adopted Rosa as his own special person. Unfortunately, she did not reciprocate his sentiments. Joe, an alcoholic who had no use for Alcoholics Anonymous, loved only his job besides Rosa, and hung out there even when he was not supposed to be working.

One day Rosa received a phone call from the owner of the bar. "Is Joe with you?" the owner asked. "We haven't seen him for days."

"No, of course not," Rosa answered. "Why should he be with me? Take a look in the little supply room out back where he sometimes hangs out with girls."

"Hold on," the owner said, and ran to check the small storage room outside the store.

After a long pause, he picked up the phone, breathing hard and saying nothing.

Rosa asked, "Well, is he there?"

"He's there all right," the owner answered. "But he isn't with any dame...He's dead."

Later Rosa received another call. "Joe's been cremated. Do you want the ashes?"

"What do I want with his ashes?" she snapped.

"Well, what *should* I do with them?"

She thought a while and said, "I know. Put them in the liquor room over in the corner. He'll be happy there for infinity. And he'll be watching over us gratefully for the rest of our lives!"

And there he rests in a dark corner of the liquor room to the present day.

November 14

I turned on the TV for a moment to check on the weather yesterday, and Woody Allen's *Hannah and Her Sisters* flashed on the screen. Of all things, Allen is obsessed in the film (and probably in life, too) with the thought of dying. "Some people want to achieve immortality through their works or their descendants," he says. "I want to achieve it through not dying." He feels he can't enjoy life if he knows he has to die. Although eager to get back to work, I became captivated by the movie and stayed to the bitter end (pun).

Allen decided to kill himself, bought a gun, and held it to his head. But leave it to a bumbler to do even that clumsily; the gun went off in a different direction. To him it was an omen that meant he should stick around for a while. He began to study Catholicism instead, and to read what the big boys like Sophocles had to say on the topic. Much like me, Allen concluded they didn't know any more than he did about it. His solution to the problem was to fall in love and get married. Ostensibly that cured him. Cured the fear of death? It would have to be one momentous love affair to cure me!

Sorry, Woody, but it's a statistical fact that women are "cured" longer than men. On the average, we can expect to live at least seven years more than the stronger sex. I frequently wonder why. There are no studies I know of that explain the discrepancy, but there is an old rumor that every ejaculation of semen takes a day off a man's life. At last, revenge for penis envy!

Sometimes I think there is no such thing as death; there is only life that stops. We are given an exciting span on earth, it stays the course for better or for worse, and then it is over. If we have a car that runs out of gas and stops running, we have no word for it; we simply say the car has come to a standstill. There is no automobile Heaven or Hell to reward or punish how good or bad the car has run. We just throw it away and get a new one. Similarly, we say the sand in the hourglass has run out; we lack a term for no more sand. So too, the notion of death tells us only that life has ended. Now you have it, now you don't. If one follows this line of thought, Freud was wrong: it is not necessary to postulate a Death Instinct; there is merely a life force that runs out.

Just as there may not be such a thing as death, modern science teaches that there is no real time, as we know it. Biological necessity has honed humankind over the millennia to see time in a linear manner as an aid to survival. Relativity theory and quantum mechanics both require that the three familiar dimensions of space be melded with a single dimension of time to form a four-dimensional space-time continuum. If time is just another dimension similar to space, the entire history of the universe from beginning to end is and always was laid out along the time line. What we normally refer to as the past still exists, as does that part of the time line we call the future. Even more important, we always have existed and will always exist in our infinitesimal sliver of the space-time continuum!

As David Darling[79] explains it, "Imagine you are sitting in a plane that is waiting to take off. The engines throttle up, the plane begins to move and you see the lights by the side of the runway flash past in sequence, just as you experience one moment after another. After the plane is airborne, however, you can look down and see all the lights together – 'at the same time.' The impression that the lights were flowing past was an illusion created by your particular position in relation to the thing you were observing."

I love contemporary science. Like religion, it can be reassuring, even if it is dead wrong! Despite my wish to believe, I am more of the mind of Rabelais[80], who said on his deathbed, "I go to seek a great Perhaps."

November 15

I just visited Ruth Dreamdigger, the dream expert and activist I wrote about in *Is There Life After Analysis?*[81] She is an unpretentious gray-haired woman who still wears her hair in the Buster Brown haircut of her childhood. I went to say goodbye because I was told she has decided to die, and has begun to eat and drink as little as possible. I found her proudly sitting up in her new electrically powered chair. She has lost a great deal of weight, and appears quite fragile, but otherwise doesn't look as close to dying as I expected. When told I knew of her plans. she nodded, as if she weren't surprised, and said in a trembling voice that she has a terrible lung disease and doesn't want to live to become a burden to her friends and caretakers. I asked how long she has had these plans.

She answered, "I first realized I was ready to die two years ago when I dreamed I was going into a brilliantly lighted room, and a huge figure seized me from the rear, clenched my arms behind me, and kept me from moving ahead. I woke up screaming so loud my friend in the next room came rushing in.

"What was terrifying to me was not dying but being kept from doing so."

"I guess you weren't ready to go yet," I said. "In fact, you don't look ready now, either."

She nodded again, and said, "That's right; I have things to do first. I have to write many friends, and I want to add a final chapter to an autobiography I wrote for my family."

I wish I could read it now.

I told her about a memory I have of her. We were at a meeting of a women's group, when she made a somewhat disagreeable comment to me. Later that day she called me up. "I want to apologize," she said.

"For what?"

"I thought over the nasty remark I made to you and decided I said it because I'm jealous of you. Here you are having two successful careers, and I don't have any!"

Ruth said laughingly, "I don't remember saying that at all."

I remember. How could anyone forget the largess of a person who could admit to such a feeling!

"Are you afraid to die? I am," I said.

"Not at all," she answered. "I've had a good life. I have lovely children; I've been active in wonderful causes and know I have influenced many people for the good. I have done what I wanted to do in life, and now I am finished. I don't believe in life after death. I think this one is it. But I believe that energy is never lost. We will all go back into the universe, and I will become one with the trees, the flowers, the sea."

I kissed her goodbye and said, "This may sound awful, but I wish for you to have what you want."

"It's not awful at all," she said. "It's wonderful."

As I got to the door she raised her quivering voice and said, "Don't be afraid to die! You will be remembered."

November 16

Dr. Margaret Ray, my dear friend of over forty years, is a woman quite different from Ruth Dreamdigger. I interviewed Margaret on how she deals with the aging process. She is a psychoanalyst still in private practice, although she is now eighty-three years old. She and I went to analytic school together and have been close friends ever since. She is always available for a friend in need, and I can't count the times I've found her advice indispensable. She is totally nonjudgmental, and accepts anything I might say as understandable. My favorite joke about her is that if I said, "Peggie, I've just killed my mother," she would answer, "I'm sure you had good reason!" A slight, gray haired, active woman, Margaret maintains a life almost as full as it ever was. She is a wonderful example of how to enjoy life in old age.

Alma: What is aging like for you, Margaret?

Margaret: Well, it's better than the alternative. Being with you makes me realize how much I have let go. Like the swimming. There was a time when I would just swim and swim and swim. Now I don't care to, I'm not sure why. I used to be a water baby. Now I don't have the lung capacity. To scuba dive way down below the waves made me feel like I was on a nursing bottle. If I swim now it only makes me realize how much I've lost. It's like walking. I can't walk as fast as I used to. This interview reminds me that I was much more active until recently in substituting activities that I could do for those I can't. I climbed steep cliffs a few years ago when I went to Nova Scotia. I can still walk for miles, but the climbing makes me breathless. When I went to Alaska I took all those side trips like walking on glaciers.

Another negative aspect is the dimming of some of my senses. My hearing is less than it used to be, so I wear a hearing aid. Of course the fact that my vision is so impaired is related to a disease process of the eye that started many years ago, so I guess I can't blame that on aging. Then there is the diminution of my strength. I can't lift as heavy weights as I used to.

Memory is sometimes tricky, so I try to rehearse some of what I've just heard so I can remember it. When you've forgotten something, the only thing to do is stop and let it go and it will come back to you. For instance, I'll start to do something and get there and then realize I didn't do what I'd intended to. Maybe I wanted to go into the next room and pick something up, nothing terribly important. But when I get there, I see something else that reminds me of a task I'd neglected to do. So I immediately pick that up and do it. Then when I finish I remember, "Oh! I came in here to get a pair of scissors." So I have to retrace my steps.

Alma: Did you go through a mourning process for what you've lost?

Margaret: I'll say. You have to grieve for each ability that goes. But you can't stay in that mourning process forever. My brother Dick says the whole process of aging is one of adaptation, compensation, finding new ways to do the things you used to do so easily. But you still do them. You never stop moving. Your body, your mind, your soul. There are changes, too, in regard to attitudes. As time goes on, things don't assume such tragic or enormous proportions. I don't get as irritated or upset with people as I used to, with their limitations or their rigidities. I think my analysis and continuing self-analysis did a lot for that. There are fewer things that outrage me. I'm still infuriated by insensitivity and cruelty. I certainly feel frustrated when I run into resistances that refuse to change or to resolve some of the hatreds that people have.

Alma: Has your body changed?

Margaret: Oh, yes. Muscles are less supple and not as strong. My balance is not the same as it used to be. What do I do about that? I just have to be aware of it and anticipate. If I'm leaning one way I have to compensate and lean back in the opposite direction. I'm going to try Tai Chi-they say that improves the balance. I've never fallen, I'm very careful. If I lose my balance I try to recapture it right away.

Alma: Do you look the same?

Margaret: NO! I have wrinkles and sags and everything like that. One thing I'm grateful for. I've never relied upon good looks and beauty; it never became a passport for me, so that the loss of smooth face and all that is not as terrible as it would be if I had been a beautiful person. I've always relied on developing skills and expanding knowledge, and that's what I keep doing. I want to learn new things all the time. I'm learning a new skill on the computer; In the last two years I've been trying to master all the

111

different programs in the software and the computer. And I've learned a lot. Now I go online and use the internet and the Web. But I'm just not skilled at it yet. (We laugh).

Alma: How does the aging process affect your relationships?

Margaret: When I was younger I was able to let go of relationships much easier than I can now, even those that aren't terribly significant. Family, intimate friends almost like family, then casual friends are the order of significance. I think it's only the most external ring I can let go of now, not the others-they are more important to me. I think I've become much more tolerant of my friends' and family's differences from me. I kind of like those differences now. It adds zest to life.

Alma: Is old age a time of growth for you, as well as loss?

Margaret: Yes, that is what makes it possible to age without bitterness, if you keep growing in any ways you can. Of course some things are physiologically impossible. I'm much more interested in other people than I used to be. That's a growth. I think the major thing about aging without too much suffering and grief is to focus on what you can and might do, and not dwell on the losses of physical ability and strength. If you hang on to what you can do, I think that is good. That's what my brother does, you have to keep moving.

Alma: What about you makes you able to age so well?

Margaret: Stubbornness for one thing, I don't give up so easily. Curiosity is another, maintaining interest in the world. Some of the processes of aging make it easy to do that, to become less judgmental, less rejecting of anyone different from you. To be receptive to who they are, unless of course they are actively hurting you or being deliberately cruel.

I think you have to appreciate what you've got as much as possible, although you can't expect to be as lithe or as strong as you were. But you can expect to make yourself as healthy as you can, by exercise, diet, and keeping your muscles as flexible, fluid and strong as possible. I hate to give up anything I was able to do, but making this dress was really a chore! (She shows me a beautiful rose colored party dress, long and graceful, that she has made. Whereas it formerly would have taken her a week or two to make it, its creation now required many months. Since she is legally blind, she has to examine every stitch through a magnifying glass. But she did make the dress! And it is as lovely as it ever would have been. What a wonderful metaphor for her life!)

I have a lot to learn from Peggie, who is able to overcome her mourning for losses brought about by aging and enjoy the abilities she has left. As short a time as ten years ago, I was a runner who won several medals in ten kilometer races around Central Park in New York. This morning my friend Lois and I went on a three and a half walk\run race for Crime Stoppers in Key West. The temperature was in the nineties and the humidity even worse. I knew I couldn't run the distance, so we walked the three and a half miles. But it made me sad to see the runners whizzing by, and to realize I probably never would run in a race again. Unlike Peggie, the dejection I felt at my loss of potency kept me from enjoying what I <u>could</u> do. After all, I *did* finish the three and a half mile course. It didn't make me feel any better that our friend Tom joked with his pals, "Where are Lois and Alma? Let's send a taxi for them!"

November 18

My reading is focusing more and more on death and aging. I read May Sarton's last journal[82], and found it made me even more depressed. When she suffered a small stroke and walked with a slight limp on her right side, Sarton realized she was making a radical transition into old age and approaching death. Most discouraging is that she lost interest in writing paper and pens, and found her beloved books a nuisance and a bore. Her anger even surfaced when a reader sent her a book to be autographed, complaining that she had to go to the post office to pick it up, unwrap it, wrap it, and return it to the post office for remailing. I personally would be delighted to have people send me books for autographing. Nor have I lost interest in pens and paper, although lately only my family, the few old friends who are left, and anything relating to books and writing completely absorb me. I blanch at the thought that I could lose even these narrow interests, which for me, like Sarton, would be the hallmark of approaching death.

Sarton also found herself growing increasingly frustrated, and began to cry because her electric can opener wouldn't work. Funny, mine isn't working either, but I've not yet begun to cry about it. But I find myself increasingly discouraged by petty details about housekeeping. Every dish I clear off the table leaves me grumbling. Is it because old age depletes one's energy, or that one resents squandering even a crumb of the dwindling remains?

My reaction to Sarton's book makes me wonder (again) if keeping a death journal is a mistake. If her book depresses me, why should I continue my journal? It is even more concentrated on death and dying than hers. Oh, well, I suppose I can always stop.

Recently I discussed a strange experience with my friend, June. I was coming home to Key West on the bus one night from a visit with my daughter Janet in Parkland and had briefly nodded off. Looking out the window, my head swirled. The scenery was totally different from what it should have been. There were overpasses that looked unfamiliar, and none of the usual landmarks were visible. At first I thought I had gotten on the wrong bus, but then distinctly remembered the conductor saying Key West as he took my ticket. Then I puzzled about whether I had fallen asleep for longer than I thought, and if the bus was much farther along its route than I expected. A glance at my watch quickly dispelled that idea. I sat there in terror, with fantasies going through my mind that some evil magic had changed the scenery beyond all recognition. I questioned whether I was losing my mind.

This is not how Key West looks, I thought. And then the light broke. Key West? But we are not in Key West. We are leaving Miami going to Key West! If one accepts the supposition that I was leaving Key West, I was right. The scenery was completely different. What was wrong was my original premise.

When I told the error to June, five years my senior, she exclaimed, "But exactly the same thing happened to me

114

last week! I was driving my car to ------, and going the right way to get there. It was only after a while I realized that I really wanted to go to -------, which is in the opposite direction. I think it is part of getting old, that our brains are short circuited in some way."

Whatever the reason for our mistakes, I hate it, I hate it, I hate it! But I must say, the aging process has its interests. You can never tell what will come or go next.

Still I keep on ruminating about what keeps me alive when so many people my age or younger have died. My e-mail friend Dorothy Beach wrote, "How do you manage to do so well, considering you don't feel you had the greatest of backgrounds?"

I wrote back, "I think I am (relatively) normal because of good genes which have endowed me (if I may be so arrogant) with a certain amount of intelligence, imagination, and good looks. The intelligence gave me a love of reading, my inspiration and solace to the present day, and led to marvelous careers as psychoanalyst and writer. imagination provided me with a rich fantasy life which helped me survive disappointments and provided my first lessons in writing. My appearance brought forth a slew of swains who loved and admired me. I am so unassertive where men are concerned that I think if they hadn't come after me, there would be no Zane, Janet, Jonny, Rachel, Mia, Jason, Alex, and Matthew. Then where would I be today? And leave us not forget psychoanalysis, which resolved many of my conflicts and helped me become the happy person I usually am. Then add a strong dose of plain good luck, and perhaps literary talent and ambition, which provide the rod and staff of my seventies."

Why *do* we all age so differently? How come some people are old at fifty and others still sailing along in their late nineties or later? I believe that in addition to our genes, we take from each stage of life something that either helps us to age successfully or contributes to our early deterioration. Dr.Louis A. Gottshalk[83] agrees that various stages in development contribute to the manner in which we manage our senescence.

I believe every stage of life gave me certain pleasures

and strengths that have come to my assistance in the aging process. A difficult infancy taught me that pain and despair will pass; latency brought me reading, the joy of a lifetime, a rich fantasy life, and the love for and of my teachers; adolescence let me know I could survive when my body and the world around me seemed to be disintegrating; young adulthood taught me the pleasures of advanced learning, as I acquired new friends of my own level of intelligence. My mid-twenties blessed me with the love of my husband, and my life's delight, my children. My thirties brought me to psychoanalysis, and my forties awarded me a Ph.D. from Columbia University and my first publication, *Sadomasochistic Patterns in an Eighteen-Month-Old Child*[84]. In my fifties, I reveled in the gratification of an increasingly successful career as a psychoanalyst and teacher. My sixties saw the birth of Rachel, Alex, and Mia, my first grandchildren, publication of my first book, *Who Killed Virginia Woolf?* and a step toward retirement in order to write. My seventies, which further enriched me by the birth of my grandsons, Matthew and Jason, center about a life in Key West, where my dream of being a full time writer has come true. The decade has seen the publication of eight books and numerous articles in professional journals and newspapers and magazines. Since satisfactions have accompanied each decade, I can only hope that the ability to find and develop new ones will enable me to experience as rich and successful an old age.

November 24

I read in *Psychologist*Psychoanalyst* that Dr. Magda Denes died last year. My reaction was quite different from what I feel at the death of friends, or people like Kennedy or old movie stars I care about. When I learned about Magda's demise, I smiled. Isn't that awful? She was ten years younger than I, and in appearance, could have been my sister. I heard her give an excellent presentation years before and consulted her professionally for a problem I don't recall now, but had to do with the aging process. To my surprise and disappointment, she was not at all helpful. She responded with, "You are an old woman. You have to accept that. Not an aging woman, or someone who is getting old, but old." And I was all of fifty-five at the time! So when I heard she was dead, an icy trickle of satisfaction slid down my esophagus. "Hah," I thought, "now we see who is the old woman! I must be doing something right that she didn't." When I deliberate on why I am still alive, my conclusion is always the same, that my desire to write, to have millions of readers emptying the shelves of the bookstores, to make the best seller list, to be awarded a Pulitzer Prize, is the Lilith that forever beckons me onward. Apparently Magda Denes had no such Lilith, or I believe she might still be alive.

My nasty smile when I read that Magda is dead reminds me of a bit of philosophy that has helped me many times in dealing with hostile or unpleasant people. I often think, "Don't be angry with him (her, them, it), and make a scene or eat yourself up with rage. Life itself will do worse damage to them than you possibly could dream of. You only have to wait long enough and you certainly will get your revenge." It works every time!

Magda sounded good and I sounded bad when we met. But I came to that conclusion too soon. As Sophocles said[85], "Don't judge a life good or bad (or healthy) before it ends." A patient or a writer either.

But when I reread Thomas Gray's *"Elegy Written in a Country Church Yard[86],"*

The boast of heraldry, the pomp of pow'r,
And all that beauty, all that wealth e'er gave,
Awaits alike th'inevitable hour
The paths of glory lead but to the grave.

it makes me wonder if I am squandering my last few precious years for a mess of porridge. But then Gray could afford to think as he did, with his Elegy written in 1751 still considered one of the greatest poems ever written!

November 25

Janet and I had a talk as we were driving to a performance of *The Barber of Seville*, at the Florida Grand Opera Company where we have a season subscription.

"Janet," I said, "I think you should hold on to the tickets after this."

"Why, Mom?"

"Well, something might happen to me so that I couldn't attend a performance."

"You could always mail me the tickets."

"Well, maybe I couldn't. I might be dead."

"Oh Mom, if I heard you died do you think I would go to the opera?"

We both began to laugh, as I said, "I never thought of that."

Then, as if she'd been waiting on cue, Janet said, "How do you see yourself living, when you get really old, Mom? Do you think you'd like a retirement home, like the one Uncle Emil lived in?"

I shuddered, as I recalled York House in Philadelphia, the huge complex for the aged my ninety-seven-year-old uncle had lived and died in. The building was nice enough, rather like a large hotel. There was even a small kitchen in his room, although he took all his meals in the common ground floor dining room. I would hate to eat all my meals with strangers, some of whom I'd probably get to dislike. In my experience, there is always at least one person in any crowd who becomes an irritant. Uncle had a roommate who slept most of the time. Emil, perhaps, ignored the man after a while, but I would be annoyed at his constant presence. Most of all, I dreaded even thinking about the halls lined with crippled and helpless old people. They just sit there and sit there. How can they not find something, anything, to do?

Oh, come on, Alma, a little voice inside of me popped up. When you are blind and deaf and crippled, you won't know what to do with yourself either!

You're probably right, little voice. But I hope I never find out first hand! Like Robert Lowell, "May I die at night/ With the semblance of my senses\ Like the full moon that fails[87]."

"What are you daydreaming about, Mom? You never answered my question," Janet said.

"I was thinking of the old Oriental proverb, 'May the tailor die with the thread between his teeth.' For me, with the pen in my hand."

Janet smiled. "Well, what do you think you *would* like if you get too old to write?" she persisted, as if she had made up her mind before she came that we would have this discussion.

"I would *like* to die like my grandfather. He kept all his wits and his vigor, and then one day when he got to be ninety-two, he just didn't wake up. I would *like* to be strong and healthy like him until the day I die, and then I want to pass away in my sleep."

A new perspective on my grandfather, a man who walked miles every day to the end of his life and who never gave up his interest in living. He remains alive in my psyche sixty years after his death. I hope I can be as healthy a model for those who follow me as he is for me. (Who served as a model for you, Grandfather, in 1850, in the days of Queen Victoria?) For the first time I felt a glimmer of consolation that in some small way I too may be alive after I die, in my children, my grandchildren, and possibly generations to come.

Janet nodded. "Yes, that would be the best way to go, as your grandfather did. I wish I had known him! But-what if you were ill or really feeble, the way some old people get, and couldn't take care of yourself?"

A few years ago I met my former analyst in the street. When I'd gone to Gisa Barinbaum for analysis, she was a strong, domineering woman who stood up before mobs and spoke her mind, not caring who if anyone she'd offended. She had escaped from a Nazi concentration camp in Germany, and I believe she wasn't afraid of anyone or anything. But when I met her near her bank on eighty-sixth Street that day, she was a broken down old woman who was terrified because her helper hadn't come for her as planned. She was afraid she would fall and get hurt, and begged me to take her home.

Speak about resolution of the transference! All patients should meet their former analysts after they have gotten old and feeble! But who is to say I won't age like Gisa? I hate to believe it, but if it can happen to a proud, powerful woman like her, it can happen to anyone.

As I talked with Janet, I remembered that after my

car accident I had a wonderful, loving nurse named Milly. We laughed and played together so that my convalescence was actually pleasant. We ate lots of *Lite and Lively* chocolate ice cream and pretzels. Once when I couldn't sleep, Milly sat there at four A.M. while I rode my exercycle. I said to her, "When I get old and senile, will you come and take care of me?"

Milly said yes.

"I'd like Milly to come and take care of me, if it comes to that. Or a reasonable facsimile," I said.

November 27

Speaking of the end of the road, I've changed my mind about *Ars moriendi.* In *Going the Distance*, by running guru George Sheehan[88], the description of his own death was so heartrending, so breathtakingly beautiful, that I, as a bottom-of-the-barrel disciple of the great champion, wept on reading it. His parting was a gift to his family they will carry around as long as they live. Would we all do as well in our last race? Tim, one of Sheehan's fourteen children, wrote:

Dad was always a great finisher; he always advised starting slowly and finishing well. He finished this race well. But not typically. This time as he approached the finish he didn't dive. He didn't reduce his consciousness to the length of a stride. He slowed down and reached back. He took my mother's hand, and he took all of our hands. We all crossed the line together, fourteen abreast, stretched out as far as the eye could see on either side. It was so beautiful.

November 30

Someone else died who has long interested me. Pamela Harriman, the United States ambassador to France. As when John F. Kennedy, Jackie Onassis, George Sheehan, and movie stars such as Bette Davis left us, the world for me is now a little poorer. U.S. Secretary of State Madeleine Albright said in a ceremony of remembrance in Paris, "With the passing of her star, this city of lights is a little dimmer."

Harriman was a fascinating woman. In addition to her brilliant career, she was one of those rare women like

Alma Mahler who become serial wives or mistresses of great men. I first learned about her when she was the companion of Adlai Stevenson. If I recall correctly, she was with him when he died. Her list of husbands reads like a "Who's Who" of her times, beginning with Winston Churchill's son Randolph, followed by famed Broadway producer Leland Hayward, and the elderly diplomat and governor of New York, Averell Harriman. The men in her life also included CBS founder William Paley and Edward R. Murrow, purported to be the love of her life.

What do these female companions of the great have that transports them to such vicarious heights? (Do any of them give lessons?) How did this woman, reported by a biographer as dumpy and frumpy, a banal milkmaid, a little plump, certainly not beautiful, manage to do it? Apparently it wasn't her intellect or sense of humor that contributed to her phenomenal success. Smith reports, "She was a woman of limited intelligence and education....whose utterances were neither witty nor memorable[89]." Her second husband, Leland Hayward, may well have answered my question when he proudly pronounced Pamela the courtesan of the century[90]. I forget who asked, "What tricks did she have, to be so successful with men?" The answer was, "She had no tricks, only enthusiasm!"

Her life reads like a fairy tale. She was born the daughter of an English baron, and soon embarked on her fabulous series of amatory and marital adventures. After becoming an American citizen she married Harriman, a pillar of the Democratic Party, and became a prominent fixture in politics as well as in Washington society. She was a key Democratic Party and Clinton-Gore campaign fund-raiser before her appointment to the Paris embassy after the 1992 election.

Perhaps the most interesting facet of Pamela's personality is that she never stopped growing. For most of her life her pattern was to take on the identity and primary preoccupation of the principal man in her life. With Churchill, it was politics, with Hayward the theatre, and with Harriman the political and international scene. After Harriman died when Pamela was sixty-five years old, she

121

developed her individuality perhaps for the first time. Now the grand possessor of her own power and fortune, she remained committed to the world of politics. When she joined the prestigious Century Association in 1990, she listed her profession as politician. She didn't find it necessary to take on the identity of Carter Brown, the director of the National Gallery of Art, who became the next leading man in the saga of Pamela Digby Churchill Hayward Harriman. Brown taught Pamela a great deal about art, and advised her to add such works as John Singer Sargent's *Stairway in Capri* to her personal collection. Although she adopted art as an avocation, in contrast to her metier with former lovers, she never allowed Brown's passion to take over her personality[91]. Pamela Harriman tended the gardens of many men during her long and enterprising lifetime, but she herself was a flower that didn't bloom until her seventies, when she became secure enough to stand alone for the first time.

There is a vast difference in estimates of Ms. Harriman's abilities. According to Sally Bedell Smith's harping biography[92], the accomplishments of Ms. Harriman were primarily the ability to make cozy with rich and influential people, predominately men. After Smith in a spiked twist of the knife writes that her subject's talents as a gadfly outstripped any others she might have possessed, she describes "the final painful spectacle of her gropings toward respectability-an ambition which culminated in her appointment as an ambassador."

"A lot of French were puzzled," Smith quotes an anonymous (!) source.

On the other hand, people as prominent as Madeleine Albright made such statements as, "She was a central figure in the history of this century. She pursued President Clinton's highest priority-to forge a Europe that would be, for the first time, fully united, fully secure and fully free." French President Jacques Chirac praised Harriman as a great ambassador of the United States and a grand lady: "She was a beautiful ambassador, probably one of the best since Benjamin Franklin and Thomas Jefferson." Avis Bohlen, Harriman's deputy in Paris before Bohlen

122

became ambassador to Bulgaria, spoke of her boss's wonderful gaiety of spirit as a colleague and her elegant style and charm as a diplomat, adding that "She had a fine political instinct." President Clinton called Harriman a cherished friend and praised her lifetime of singular achievement. He cited her truly indomitable spirit..."She lifted our spirits and our vision." He mentioned her support of him throughout his career, and generously said, "Today I am here in no small measure because she was there."

Which of the estimates are correct? Take your pick. I personally am sorry she is gone.

January 27

Ah, Death! I don't like it; I don't understand it; I'd rather not be reminded of it! Isabella Rossellini[93] apparently feels the same way. She writes in her autobiography (which is dedicated "To my ghosts") about her mother, Ingrid Bergman's practice of placing photographs of friends who were still alive on one window and pictures of dead friends on another. As Ingrid grew older, "the rate of those who died greatly exceeded the number of newly acquired friends....with time they (the windows) became the most ghoulish and depressing sight in the house."

I can understand Isabella's reluctance to be reminded of the death of her mother's friends and her own eventual demise. Later in the book[94], she speaks of a symbol she places on her calendar commemorating the anniversary of deaths of those close to her. She writes, "I don't know yet where my own (symbol) will be placed, but when I look at a calendar, this thought gives me a chill down my spine."

Not many of us are able to accede to the dark ogre of death as well as Ingrid Bergman. Perhaps she became the great artist she was because she dared to experience her most profound feelings without repression, as in her passion for Roberto Rossellini, and in living with the greatest pain of all, the loss of those she loved.

January 28

WHY CAN'T I WRITE? Months have gone by since my last friend died, and I've even put off scribbling in my journal. But I know the answer to my question. Kendall Kane's death is the hardest of all to bear. Joan and Anna were the friends of my youth, and Jill the adored comrade of my adolescence. But Kendall was the companion of my mature years, who shared my most intimate feelings, who accepted my ugliest thoughts as only human, who befriended me in joy and sorrow, who somehow made grief endurable. Together we interpreted our dreams, analyzed our behavior, talked of our hopes and yearnings, discussed our sex lives, our dissatisfactions and disappointments, our children, our husbands, our mothers-especially our mothers. And perhaps best of all, we laughed at ourselves when we were ridiculous. Kendall knew me better than anyone else did in the whole world and loved me anyway.

I dreamed about her again last night.

I was standing on my balcony looking down at the living room. I noticed a huge hole in the middle of the floor, and was happy to see that workmen were busily fixing it. The whole room appeared a dazzling sapphire blue, the color of the vase that was Kendall's last gift to me.

As Shakespeare wrote, "Death lies on her like an untimely frost[95]." If I write about Kendall, I will have to think about her. If I think about her, I will have to remember. If I remember, I will miss her unbearably. If I miss her, I will cry ...and cry...and cry. Dare I risk it?

Dare I not?

Well, at least I can try....

Part 10: Kendall Kane

January 29

It began in 1974 when I opened a copy of *Voices*, a small psychotherapy journal which regularly carried Kendall's work. Her article was called *The Negative Aspects of Therapeutic Change*[96]. It said that hidden among our negative facets are qualities that could make us richer and more vital people. Rather than phase them out, Kendall suggested we look inside them for unique features of our deepest selves. She wrote:

"I'm searching and changing all the time while like the river, I'm still the same. Still practice psychotherapy, still train teachers and psychologists at City College, still treasure significant relationships and am looking for more of them."

She went on to say that most therapists strive for change in their patients, and grumble or even terminate when nothing happens.

"I would like to discuss the inadvisability of striving for drastic change. Instead I wish to raise the alternative of accepting our qualities, the negative and the positive, as part of ourselves. If we could welcome and incorporate our less admirable qualities we would be richer and more vital people.

"I, like many therapists have had two 'analyses.' The first one was fairly "orthodox." Its focus was on dynamics of my personality. We considered how my past experiences contributed to my present life situation. I saw clearly my rivalry with my mother and my sisters-how my life was geared to outdoing them. I looked at my feelings of superiority, my contempt, my pretense, and I set about to resolve them. Undoubtedly, they were not 'constructive' qualities. I turned (sublimated) them into working for excellence, sharing with others in collaborative endeavors, dropping many of the games I played. I succeeded, and had what is known as an excellent 'therapeutic outcome.' The only trouble was I was so focused on being constructive that a whole lot of me was kept in tow.

"So ten years later, back to the couch I went. I was shocked that my new analyst did not expect great changes. He said he rarely experienced dramatic shifts in patients' basic structure. I never found out what he meant by this, but came to my own conclusion; I am still conscious of my limitations as well as my assets. I deplore some and rejoice in others, but feel I would be lost if I didn't have both. I am still impatient and impetuous, which prompts me to leave meetings or even friends abruptly. Sometimes I miss a great thing. Sometimes I avoid stark boredom. But that's the way I am. People ask me, 'Aren't you afraid of your destructive characteristics?' No, I'm not. As a severe neurotic I never would have killed anyone. As a freer person, killing is not to my liking either. Oh, I may hurt others, deliberately hurt them, more than I used to, but I respect them enough to know they will survive. As a matter of fact I get hurt more than I'm likely to hurt someone else. To tell you the truth, that is one quality I <u>would</u> like to change! But I am less polite than I was and people who can't take me this way are quite skilled in avoiding me. I find myself surrounded more and more with compatible companions.

"One might argue that this is change after all. And to be sure it is, but of a different sort. It has an inclusiveness of all facets of one's nature-not a selecting of 'good' traits only. I am all of me-take it or leave it. If I were a monster I presume society would deal with me quickly enough. But since I'm simply a mercurial, kindly, humorous, amiable, agreeable, frustrated, fiery woman, I enjoy it more and worry about it less."

I come from a family of critical women, and was impressed that Dr. Kane sounded like a person who could accept weaknesses along with good points in her friends, as well as in herself. I also felt the author of the article was sending out signals of her availability for new relationships. I determined that one day I would get to know Kendall Kane.

A few months later, I went to a meeting of The American Academy of Psychotherapists in Ashville, North Carolina, to hear an expert on dreams. I didn't learn a great deal about dreams, but I met Kendall Kane. I responded much as I expected to the effervescent, charismatic Kendall, a woman with a smile worth millions who clearly was not a person to get lost in a crowd. We were intimate friends from the moment we met. At least I was; it took Kendall a few days longer. She said to me that first day, "I'm scared of you." I always intended to ask what she meant, but never got around to it. Now I will never know.

Suddenly I put down my pen to wipe away the tears that were smearing the ink in my journal. I sat there mournfully for what seemed like hours. Then I wrote, I *can't* write about Kendall any more! I don't *have* to and I'm not going to. I'm going to stop right here. So I did, writing with a flourish, "Death" takes a holiday!

I assuaged my conscience with the words of La Rouchfoucauld, "Death and the sun are not to be looked at steadily[97]."

March 21
I haven't picked up my journal again for over three months. I've been depressed since my last entry, not exactly morose, but enough that all the world seems swaddled in gray wool. I flip the pages of *The Best Seller*, a book I fully expected to enjoy, and soon realize I have no idea what it is about. I didn't even remember the name without looking it up. I walk out of hit movies like *Independence Day*. Nothing feels good to me any more; even chocolate candy has no taste. I've lost

all interest in beauty and nature. The Flame Trees outside my window seem flat as paper dolls. Although I usually wait impatiently for them to bloom, this year the brilliant orange blossoms fall on leadened eyes. I argue with anyone foolish enough to come close to me, even my sister. (Maybe especially my big sister.) I can't stand to be with anyone. But then I'm lonely, and run to whoever phones me, even if I don't particularly like the person. Then after I've said my "How are you's," I can't wait to get away. What I miss most is the good natured enjoyment of life that is usually characteristic of me.

I sit in my bedroom in front of the computer and stare at the empty screen. I know what I *should* write about, but like a stubborn child who won't eat what's good for her, I refuse. Do something, Alma! You've got to get moving, I tell myself. But what? If I only knew...

March 22

This morning I woke from a dream in which I was in an airplane strapped into a seat by a large window. I looked out the window and saw the sky was the color of ashes. All of a sudden the mist shot off like a flock of birds, and presto! the sun was revealed from behind the clouds.

Maybe the dream is predicting my emotional climate will clear up. Let's hope it's soon. I can't stand this dreary world much longer.

I *have* to write about Kendall, or I will remain in this netherworld forever. Hard as I try to push away the feeling, I have a need to write about her that won't disappear. Something of her inside me wants to come out like the sun in my dream, insists on being heard. It's as if she is lying in wait for me to conclude her story. Somehow, she *needs* me to write about her, to clear up the fog, to do for her what she is unable to do for herself. Kendall had a way of getting what she wanted. Apparently, she still does. So like it or not, back to Kendall I must go.

No! I don't want to do this! I won't! Even in jail the prisoners don't have to work if they don't feel like it. Why should I? I shouldn't. Should I?

Come on Alma, get to work.

No! I'm tired! I'll just take a little nap first.

You have to start writing!

No! I'm hungry. I think I'll make an egg-white sandwich. A little lunch will do me good.

Enough of these excuses already. Start writing!

No! I have to go to the bathroom.

You just went a few minutes ago! Start that chapter!

No! I'll watch a little TV first. I haven't seen any for weeks.

Alma!

Oh, all right. Who wants to see commercials anyway? I'll just play a Maria Callas CD. I haven't heard *La Traviata* for ages. Oh God, is she singing of loss and dying again? Forget it.

Work, damn it!

Stop pestering me!

Okay, but just open your notebook for a minute.

No! You can't make me.

Well then, run your hand back and forth over the suede beige cover. You know you love the touch of it. It feels smooth, so smooth, against your fingertips, and then turns rough as you move against the grain. It makes shivers run down your spine.

What? The hair on the back of your neck is bristling? I believe it. Kendall is trying to tell you something. She's saying, "What kind of friend are you? Just because I'm dead doesn't mean you can ignore me! It won't hurt you to do something for someone you love. It may be the last thing you'll ever be able to do for me. I'll never forgive you if you don't."

Okay, Kendall, enough already! Get off my neck. You win. For better or for worse, here goes....

March 22 (later that day)

Kendall was seven years older than I, the same age as my sister, and indeed I always looked up to Kendall as an older sibling. There was a ready made empty place inside of me that was quietly waiting for her to come along. I hadn't even known the spot was empty until I met her. Something about the way she pulled herself up to her full height made me love her. Kendall was a queen, and didn't need it corroborated. She was the kind of woman who moved with consequence, as if existence were not trivial. An animal magnetism pulled both men and women into her orbit as soon as they met her, and made everyone want to possess her. As a friend said, "Wherever Kendall sits is the head of the table." I adored this quality in her, a fullness of presence, a complete immersion of herself into the moment, and wished I had it too.

Kendall had more integrity than anyone I've ever known. After fifty years of subterfuge, manipulation, and pretense, she made up her mind (after much therapy) that she was going to devote her life to telling the truth. She determined to ignore whether her words hurt anyone, or even if it made her enemies, and say what she thought at all times. She believed such a practice avoided confusion and made for clearer lines between people.

"We are strong enough to face the truth when told it directly," she said, "especially since we sense anyway when we are being lied to."

She carved out a difficult path for herself, and although it cost her many so-called friends, it also made possible over fifteen years of intimate friendship between us. Until the end, we never had a disagreement we didn't discuss and somehow work out. "No, I don't like your new dress" was relatively easy for me to take, and I learned to live with whether Kendall liked my dress or not. But some things were a bit harder to take. I had seen a lovely amber pendant that I wanted to buy Kendall for her birthday the first year of our friendship. I put it aside in the jewelry store and wanted her to go to look at it. "I don't feel like getting a birthday present today. Don't bug me," Kendall grumbled. Although my feelings were hurt, I found her frankness refreshing and liberating, and the occasional "no" an inexpensive price to pay for the fullness of her presence. I think that was the secret of Kendall's charisma; she lived fully in the moment because she was rarely in the moment at all unless that was where she wanted to be.

The philosophy of honesty at all costs worked for Kendall, and I try to emulate her in this way of being.

Unfortunately, I don't do it well, and tend to blurt out truths tactlessly. This frequently makes me enemies, including the behaviorist head of my dissertation committee, whom I foolishly told that I didn't believe in any form of psychology besides psychoanalysis. (At that time I was encased in the theory and practice of psychoanalysis, and had no room for other forms of treatment. I have grown up a bit since.) The professor almost had me thrown out of the doctoral program, but fortunately for my future as a psychologist, was decent enough to resign from my committee. Despite such hazardous results, Kendall's teaching sank in, and remains part of me to the present day, although I'm not sure I'm always better off for it. I'm afraid that in contrast to Kendall, the ability to speak up effectively will never be one of my strong points.

Thinking of Kendall disturbed me so badly I vowed to stop thinking about her. I'll just think about my grandchildren, or my book, *Who Killed Virginia Woolf?*[98] that just went into a second printing. That should help-at least for a while. And I'll visit my friend, Rosa, who is always fun to be with.

March 23

Rosa, the first thought on my mind the next morning. I am upset about Rosa, who is ill with cancer. Her hair is falling out and she tires easily. I learned about it through her son, who let it slip that Rosa was ill. Rosa denied it, and refuses to take any medication. Instead, she goes to a quack who she professes "is spiriting away my symptoms." Rosa is a beautiful woman, proud and haughty. Although she is seventy years old, she's maintained the gorgeous figure that once made her an artist's model. Men who are young enough to be her sons still pursue her.

I surreptitiously glanced at my friend and thought she looked dreadful. Her beautiful face was lined and haggard: her color was bad, kind of grayish beige. I can't bear it, I thought. Aging, pain, despair, illness, and death. Is that what the rest of my life will be about?

I peered closely in the mirror at my own face. I was relieved to see that although we are of similar age I didn't have the same look as Rosa. To me, I appeared rested, with a natural pinkish color. I opened my eyes wide, squinted, turned my face this way and that, and saw nothing adverse except fine wrinkled lines around my eyes and mouth. That woman in the mirror looks healthy, at least for now, I told myself. But how long can it go on? I keep waiting for the recalcitrant lump, the bloody discharge, the sore spot that doesn't heal. Like Shelley[99], I worry nightly "that death like sleep might steal on me." It is just a matter of time until something strikes. After all, old age is a terminal illness....

I thought of a movie I'd seen years ago called "They Shoot Horses, Don't They?" which starred Jane Fonda. It was about a marathon dance, the kind they ran during the Depression, in which the winners won a lot of money. The contestants danced night and day as long as they could hold out, sometimes for weeks. Often one person shuffled on, carrying his sleeping partner on his feet. Sometimes a dancer was dragged around the floor by his or her partner. And occasionally both parties trudged on while asleep. But one by one each of the staggering couples dropped out, until finally only the winners remained. I think the film is a metaphor for life. Unfortunately, in the dance of life there are no final winners, but I hope to be one of the last dancers to leave the floor.

It reminds me of a time almost thirty years ago when a well known physician suspected a lump in my breast was malignant, and scheduled a biopsy three weeks later. The waiting period yawned interminably ahead. Rudy took me to his therapist, who he thought could help me deal with my anxiety. The woman took one look at me and said, "That woman doesn't have cancer!"

Three women went into surgery for biopsies that morning. One was Helen Gahagan Douglas, the liberal senator from Maine and wife of the actor, Melvin Douglas. It was shortly after she had been beaten for office in so despicable a manner by Richard Nixon. (I always held him responsible for her death.) Douglas and the other patient were diagnosed with benign breast lumps, whereas the physician insisted my tumor was malignant. I had a chronic cystic breast disease, and had gone to see him about a new lump.

"You know this one is different than the others you've had, Alma," he said.

When I came out of surgery, Rudy was sitting beside me in the recovery room. "Was it cancer?" I asked, fumbling through the bedclothes for my breast.

"No!" he said, his voice rising with exultation. "The lump was benign!"

Helen Gahagan Douglas and the other woman died of breast cancer later that year, while I am still dancing the marathon.

March 24

I had another death shock that evening after my visit with Rosa. Shocks are getting to be my daily dozen. I'd turned my computer on to Prodigy, the online service, where I enjoy reading the People section, and discovered that Marty Balsam had died at the age of seventy-six. Marty, a good friend and fellow actor of Rudy's, was a man I was fond of. What I remembered most was that I had met him forty years ago walking down Central Park West and he kissed me on the cheek. "A famous actor kissed me!" I told a friend.

According to Prodigy, Marty was found alone in a hotel room in Italy four days after he died. The news said the cause of death was unknown. I wondered if he'd killed himself. Divorced from his second wife in 1962, he had never remarried. What was such a nice man and wonderful actor doing alone in a hotel room in Europe, where nobody knew for four days if he were alive or dead? I found myself fighting little wracked gasps for most of the day.

More bad news! Bernard, my dear friend Harriet's husband, suddenly died. Harriet is another old friend from my college years. Their elegant wedding was chiefly memorable to me for Harriet's poise and joy during it; a proud bride mingling with her guests as though it were the happiest day of her life. This was not my experience nor that of most of my friends during our own weddings where we tended to be nervous wrecks, and Harriet's pleasure was borne out in her long, happy marriage. I was concerned about Harriet, whose whole life had revolved about her life's

133

companion of fifty years. When I phoned her, she said, "I don't know if I can make it alone." Will she? I wondered.

I'm looking at a snapshot taken outside my home on my college graduation day. Four smiling young women standing in a row, our arms wrapped around each another; Anna, Jill, Harriet, and me. All of my best friends at the time. Now Anna and Jill are dead, and I fear for Harriet's life.

Oh not Harriet too! I couldn't stand losing another friend.

A few weeks later I talked with Harriet. She had just come back from visiting her new grandson in Chicago, and for the first time since Bernard's death, there was a spark of joy in her voice.

"It's the first time I've felt I would ever get out of the blackness," she said. I was delighted, but thought I should warn my friend that the battle was not yet over.

"Do you know grief comes in waves, Harriet?" I asked. "For me, it always does. But it returns only temporarily. Each time the periods of sorrow grow further and further apart.

"Something is wrong with me," my reserved, dignified friend cried. "I can't remember things about Bernard, even the sound of his voice."

"Remembering him causes you pain. It won't always be that way. Some day you will remember only the pleasure you shared together." Harriet is a private person, who doesn't confide in many people. So I said, "Talk about him. Talk about him all the time. Talk about him to anyone who will listen." She did.

I sent her a poem by Terry Kettering called *The Elephant in the Room*[100] that I find moving:

> There's an elephant in the room.
> It is large and squatting, so it is hard to get
> around it.
> Yet we squeeze by with How are you? and
> I'm fine.
> And a thousand other forms of trivial chatter.
> We talk about the weather.
> We talk about work.

We talk about everything-except the
elephant in the room.
There's an elephant in the room.
We all know it is there.
We are thinking about the elephant as we talk
together.
It is constantly on our minds.
For, you see, it is a very big elephant.
It has hurt us all.
But we do not talk about the elephant in the
room.
Oh, please. say his name.
Oh, please, say Bernard again.
Oh, Please, let's talk about the elephant in the room.
For if we talk about his death,
Perhaps we can talk about his life.
Can I say Bernard to you and not have you
look away?
For if I cannot, then you are leaving me
Alone...In a room...
With an elephant.

Harriet is over seventy years old. If it is so difficult for her to accept loss, what must it be like for a bereft child, who hasn't had time to develop the fortitude to live with pain. Wendy's mother, my five-year-old grandson Matthew's other grandmother, died a year and a half ago, and the child is still mourning her. Matthew recently said, "I miss my grandmother. She read me a lot of books, and she was very nice to me. She hugged me all the time and bought me toys. I think about her very much, at special times. Like when my friends came over and she met them. She liked my friends and me. She always gave me and my friends a hug."

All I could do was to give him a hug. Unfortunately, grief begins when it needs to begin, and pays no attention to age or readiness to tolerate pain. How sad that Matthew had to lose a loving grandmother so early in his life!

June Nelson, in another of her sensitive poems, captured the grief of a child:

In Shallow Water

Standing beside me
At the shallow end of the pool
As I practiced my calisthenics
A skinny little girl
About eight years old
With bowl-cut, sun-streaked hair
Said to me, almost in a whisper,
My grandmother died.
My grandfather is very sad
We are all very sad
But we are getting over it.
She was very sick.
We loved her very much.
I miss her all the time.
The child talked on and on,
We are very sad but we are getting better.
I said nothing.
She couldn't seem to stop the flow of words
As I moved rhythmically beside her.

March 25

My book *Profiles of Key West*[101] sold a hundred copies at my book signing at the Caroline Street Bookstore, brought in a packed house when I spoke at the "Friends of the Library," and was well reviewed by the newspapers. Today is a better day. Perhaps I'm over the depression caused by all the deaths, at least temporarily. But now I have no inspiration to continue with my journal. I'm afraid it will make me feel bad again. As I told Harriet, grief comes in waves. It is only a matter of time until it returns. Or someone else will die and set it off all over again.

I was watching the scene from *La Traviata* in which Alfredo's father, Germont, informs the courtesan Violetta she must renounce Alfredo's hand, or his sister's fiancé will refuse to marry her. The betrothed is shallow, indeed, if he would give up his intended bride because of the former profession of her brother's lover.

The scene with its glorious music and heartrending libretto is one of the most beautiful in all of opera. I cry, but it makes me furious at the same time. "God will reward you for this noble act," the narrow-minded, sanctimonious fool tells Violetta. I believe everything wrong with so-called morality and religion is encapsulated in this scene, in what is really a morality play. Under the guise of nobility, Germont performs a cruel and vicious act. By taking Violetta away from her true love, he breaks two hearts, and is indirectly sentencing her to consumption and death. There is so much unavoidable loss in the world that giving up one's love for anything less than life itself is just plain stupid.

It is amazing how differently people deal with death. I had lunch with Rebecca McGowen, who lost her forty-four-year-old husband Richard less than two months ago. Rebecca is the kindly lifestyle editor of the Key West Citizen, for whom I wrote interviews last year. She'd been keeping me posted about an unusual ailment of Richard's, who'd suffered from sleep apnea which caused him to fall asleep at inopportune moments. Although he formerly was executive chef at the Marriott Hotel, it was not listed in his credits in the obituary. I guess falling asleep over the soup is not the best way to proceed in that line of business. The last time I saw Rebecca, Richard was slated to go to Miami for an intensive series of tests. I was shocked to open the newspaper and find his obituary.

When I went to his funeral service, he lay in his coffin, a slender, white-faced man, slightly balding at the temples, with a dark mustache slanting to his chin. He didn't look quite dead, nor did he seem fully alive, but as if he were temporarily suspended somewhere in between. While I was looking at him, someone moved. I jumped, thinking Richard was getting up and walking away. Wishful thinking, I decided sadly.

Rebecca is feeling better now. She isn't eating well, because Richard had prepared all their meals. But the loss of weight is becoming. She's gone through a lot of pain, but I believe her direct, honest approach is helping her survive. She is able to speak simply and openly about her grief. She went back to work at the *Key West Citizen* the week after Richard died. But a few days later, she phoned her editor-in-chief and said simply, "I need the day off. I'm not able to work today." Of course he agreed. She is learning to go to the movies herself, and even to a restaurant alone.

I couldn't help but compare the course of Rebecca's mourning with Harriet's, who lost her husband about the same time. Harriet's life had revolved around Bernard for fifty years. Rebecca is much younger than Harriet, and has a life of her own apart from her marriage. I believe the richer one's life is outside of the relationship with the beloved, the easier it is to compensate for his or her loss. But as Harriet discovered when she visited her grandchild, the healthy mourner eventually learns there is life beyond grief. This lesson is the beginning of recovery.

March 26

It is four A.M. and I can't sleep. I'm thinking about all my things and what will become of them after I die. What will happen to the mountain of books I've collected all my life? My bookshelves cover the walls. I have thousands of volumes, beginning with the five paperbacks bought in 1939 when they first came out. They contain the *Tales from Shakespeare* volume Anna gave me for my birthday. I remember the excitement with which I greeted those first paperbacks. They sold for a quarter then. A whole book, and only twenty-five cents! Somehow I sensed what that meant, a harbinger of the paperback revolution to come. How great a movement I couldn't foresee, but the excitement of the adolescent Alma is reflected in the millions of paperbacks sold since.

A wise patient of mine once said, "Our books are growing old along with us." Some of mine are over sixty years old. The leaves have turned yellow and sometimes when I pick up a book fragile little pieces fall out. I bought *A Passage to India*[102] when I was in college, and kept it-unread-until I was sixty years old and Rudy and I stopped in India on our way around the world. The book shed little yellow fragments all over the globe. The remaining pages were held together with a rubber band. But how wonderful to have had the book when I needed it, even if I had to wait fifty years!

I've willed my extensive library of psychoanalytic

books to *The Institute for Psychoanalytic Training and Research,* where I trained and taught. But so many members are aging it is possible the Institute will be inundated with ancient classics and not want mine at all. I once asked a colleague if members over sixty-five no longer had to pay dues. He snorted and said, "If people over sixty-five stop paying dues, we'll have no money at all in the coffer!"

What about the stacks and stacks of beloved novels, some with broken backs, now drooping with age? I know what will happen to the ones the libraries don't want. My son-in-law Sam is my executor. Sam has a mania for getting rid of clutter. The books will be thrown out in the garbage. Perhaps the "Friends of the Library" in Key West will have an Alma Bond book sale. Then, if I am lucky, my lovingly collected books will sell for twenty-five cents apiece.

Many newspaper and magazine articles I have written are stuck haphazardly among my books. I can see them being thrown out, too, as nobody will realize they were written by me. I guess that's why I was so happy to have Poho Press publish *Profiles of Key West,* which consists of twenty-nine of the favorite interviews I wrote for newspapers. It is a little harder to overlook a book than yesterday's newspaper articles, already destined to be thrown out with the garbage or used to wrap fish.

"Janet," I complained to my daughter, "nobody will realize that some of the books, magazines, and newspapers contain articles and reviews written by me. When I die they will be thrown out!"

"Put them all on a shelf labeled Alma's writing," Janet retorted.

"Great idea," I said. "Why didn't I think of that?"

Excess books are not a new problem for me. When I moved from New York to Key West, I gave away eighty-eight boxes of them. I don't even remember to whom I gave most of them. But my extensive art collection went to the library of Bucharest in Romania, because a fire had destroyed their entire book collection. I donated them in honor of my mother, who was born there. And Rudy's theatre books went to a friend who owns a drama school.

And what about all my photographs, many of them

lying about in unsorted piles? Lots of the subjects will be unrecognized by anyone after I am gone. Some of them *I* don't even recognize. I know. Into the garbage will go pictures of my mother, father, aunts and uncles, unknown infants and childhood friends, along with many of the clothes, shoes, and artifacts I brought back from all over the world. Again Janet came to the rescue. "We'll go through all your piles of pictures and label them." So she took them home and she and Sam did a wonderful job of pasting the hundreds of photos in albums. They are a joy to have and to look at again and again. Too bad I won't be around long to enjoy them!

Nobody will know that the little painted birds came from an airport in Austria, my Persian rugs from India and China, that the black clay plates with Greek myths sculpted on them cost three cents apiece on Crete thirty-five years ago. Or that Rudy bought me the painted wooden dolls on top of Mt. Fujiami. Or that the bright red and yellow wooden statue of a woman was carved by a Balinese and purchased by me for one dollar on the beaches of Bali.

Precious memories of my travels to Bali, to Russia, to China, to Japan, to Thailand, to the British Isles, to Hong King, to Shanghai, to France, to Italy, to Alaska, to Romania. I often run my fingers over each item and remember the countries they came from. But to those who come after me, the articles will have no more value than the stuff picked up for a few dollars in Pier One. Into the garbage they will go, along with my books and other treasures. No wonder people don't want to die. Who wants to think of their beloved possessions buried in the greasy mound of Mt. Trashmore?

For some reason I thought of Phil Gallob, the only accountant I used for almost forty years. I recently received a letter from him saying he had an advanced case of Parkinson's Disease and was forced to retire. It is only a matter of time until he dies. I sent him a letter, which said,
I am so sorry you are ill and retiring, Phil. In all the years of my career I've never used the services of another accountant. What will s/he do with my two shopping bags full of receipts and old checks? Who was pleased to watch my income go up every year I was in practice, and went through the rigors of

two audits without falling apart or letting me collapse? Who struggled for years trying to make sense of actor Rudy's and my ridiculously complicated joint forms? What other accountant will be interested that I've started to make a little money from my writing? We've been through more than half of my lifetime together, Phil, and another CPA just won't be the same!

March 28

I dreamed I was buying a new sofa for my living room. The sofa was black with gray sections in it. Shirley's husband, Timothy, was in the dream, although I didn't see his face. I realized I couldn't buy the couch yet because it wasn't being sold for a while. I WOULD HAVE TO WAIT.

At first I thought the dream was a romantic one about Dr. Timothy Syms, whom I'd never met, but who sounded like a considerate and generous husband. But then I realized that black is the color of grief, and Timothy is in mourning.

I cannot sit on that couch yet. It is a couch of death and it is too soon for me to "buy" it. The time is not yet ripe. Indeed, I will have to wait. A relieving dream!

Then I had another dream.

I was on the beach, while my sister Pauline is swimming with my granddaughters. I want to join them, but do not have my red bathing cap. I go to the next beach to find it, and when I get back they have left. It is too late for me to join them.

I guess that's the story of my life now. It is too late for "swimming" once more in the ocean of love. I believe the swimming in the dream is a symbol of my sister's exciting marriage, I suppose in some ways richer than mine, and I hope the little girls will one day, too. But there won't be any more "swimming" for me. It is too late.

I read about a woman who found out she had the gene for Huntington's disease. She said the worst part of it was knowing she was sitting on a time bomb. It was only a matter of time until it went off. I too am sitting on a bomb and it is only a matter of time, perhaps any minute, perhaps twenty-five years from now, until it explodes. Will I die from

141

a cerebral hemorrhage like the one that killed my mother? Every slight ping in the head brings terror with it. Will I be struck down by a heart attack like Rudy's? Is that muscular strain in my shoulder a disguised heart ailment? Will I die of diverticular bleeding as my father did? A family ailment. Will I develop Alzheimer's like Jill, and lead a deplorable existence that isn't any life at all? And with no Barry to sweeten my final days. Or will I peacefully pass away in the night like my grandfather, who never knew what it was that hit him? I should be so lucky.

This brooding about death is keeping me from enjoying the little time I have left. And yet in some ways it is a good thing to face. There is nothing sadder than those little old ladies who walk around New York City with heavily rouged cheeks, wearing colored gauzy rags. As Jill once said when I asked why she had cut her corn colored shoulder length hair, "When I turn around, men are disappointed. I don't want that to happen. I prefer that they not expect anything sexier."

Why can't I forget my age, and just go on living as if life were eternal? Lots of older people do. When I told Harriet that many of my friends had died, and that we'd better get together while there was still time, she said, "Well, don't worry about me. I'm planning to be around for a long time." I hope she will be, but she'd better not count on it. I suggested she do whatever it is she wants to do today, as there aren't too many tomorrows left. Others have told me they don't give dying a thought; it's what happens to other people, not them. As Shakespeare said[103], "Men shut their doors against a setting sun."

Shakespeare's line gives a superb interpretation of one of my first dreams about death:
I was moving into a new apartment. It wasn't as pretty as my present house. I opened a neighbor's door and saw a decrepit old woman inside. I hastily shut the door.

Now I feel more the way the mother of Joanna, a former patient of mine, did. Joanna said they didn't have to go see an exhibition at the Metropolitan immediately, because it was permanent.

"Yes, but we're not permanent," her mother replied.

142

I do understand why I can't forget about my age and go on about my life. This has not always been true of me. Like many others, I used to deny the facts to preserve the notion that calamity befalls only others. People need time to absorb the profound implications of the catastrophe that has befallen them. A good example is the reaction of Christa McAuliffe's mother on January 28, 1986, when she viewed the accident that killed her daughter and the entire crew of the United States space shuttle Challenger, seventy-three seconds after it took off from the Kennedy Space Center. The disaster left a snakelike cloud of smoke twisting through the skies that no one who saw could ever forget. The tragic mother was photographed as she looked up at the smoke, asking, "What is that?"

Despite my early history of denials, I can't permanently repress the forewarning of my own death. Untimely experiences with my husband, brother, son, and friends have ripped the protective blinders from my eyes in regard to my own demise. But I don't regret dealing with the subject now. For one thing, it is inspiring me to write this journal, which is helping me to cope with my losses. Although denial is a normal self-protection that enables us to go about our lives, those who wish to be artists have to learn to look truth in the eye to seed the creative process. I only wish I had learned this earlier in my life.

The great Austrio-German composer and conductor Gustav Mahler was able to face his fears of death, and sublimate them in his magnificent Ninth Symphony, which reflects his preoccupation with death[104]. It was the composer's last complete work and symbolizes his farewell to the world[105]. Although Mahler was brave enough to confront his terror of dying, he was superstitious about calling his symphony Number Nine, because Beethoven died right after finishing his ninth. Perhaps it was a premonition of tragedy, for the subject of Mahler's Ninth worried his wife. Soon their little daughter became ill with scarlet fever and died. This was a repetition of Mahler's sad childhood, when only six of fourteen siblings survived to maturity. Shortly after his daughter's death, the grieving Mahler became ill with heart disease. An uneven rhythm in the first movement of the Ninth suggests his failing heartbeat. According to Lewis Thomas[106], the symphony, especially the final movement, is an open acknowledgment of death. Thomas interprets the string passages at the end as Mahler's concept of leave-taking. In a short passage near the conclusion of the fourth movement, the instruments of the orchestra drop out one by one, and reflect the composer's thoughts about dying. The almost vanishing violins are edged aside for a few bars by the cellos, which pick up fragments from the first movement, as though prepared to begin everything all over again. Lewis sees this as a wonderful few seconds of encouragement: we'll be back, we're still here, keep going, keep going...

My friend June Nelson understands the importance for the creative process of avoiding the defense mechanism of denial. She wrote this lovely poem after the death of her husband:

The Quiet Place
It is a beautiful quiet place
On a gentle hill
The old stones mossy and crumbling
The fresh granite of new ones
Glistening in the sun.
But she hates this place
Hates the fresh green rectangle
Hates the tell-tale bright new stone.
It makes it all too real.
He is gone deep in the ground
In this place.
She visits rarely.
Friends think her unloving.

Always proud and arrogant
Facing reality head-on
But now when she is in her kitchen
Cutting up carrots and celery
She feels he is in the other room
Working quietly at his desk.

144

I had dinner with a man the other night who was obsessively interested in discussing the subject of death. When I said the fear of death is universal, he disagreed. He said he's had a good life and therefore has no fear of death. Repeatedly stressing that he is ready to go at any time, he insisted he would have no regrets. He believed himself, but I didn't believe him. If he was correct in his affirmation, why did he find it necessary to go on and on about his lack of fear? A short while later, I heard that my friend had been diagnosed with prostate cancer. Ernest Becker[107] says "...everything man does in his symbolic world is an effort to deny and overcome his grotesque fate. He literally drives himself into a blind obliviousness with social games, psychological tricks, personal preoccupations so far removed from the reality of his situation that they are forms of madness-agreed madness, shared madness, disguised and dignified madness, but madness all the same." Indeed, there is a growing body of research, including psychological tests which measure galvanic skin responses that bear out the hypothesis that fear of death lies deep within every one of us. According to Fritz Perls[108], the fear of death "is the layer of our true and basic animal anxieties, the terror that we carry around in our secret heart." Only when we explode it can we "get to the layer of our authentic self: what we really are without sham, without disguise, without defenses against fear."

My mother fainted when she was told her son was dead. The reality was unbearable, and fainting gave her a few moments of blessed peace. But I don't have the luxury of being able to deny that my stay on earth is shrinking by the moment. The protective mechanism was punctured for me when my hitherto healthy eighteen-year-old brother was struck down with cerebral meningitis and died, and again when my beloved, emotionally sound son Zane developed bipolar disease. Kendall's death was the final note that taught me too well that tragedy can strike us or our loved ones as easily as it befalls others. Despite Freud's dictum that man cannot accept the idea of his own death, I *know* I will die relatively soon. Perhaps if I prepare for it, it won't take me by surprise.

April 1

Well, now that I've explained why denial doesn't work for me anymore, let's get on with the saga of Kendall Kane. It's going to hurt, but it hurts anyhow. So I might as well write about it.

I never understood how Kendall got to be the woman she was. The third of three daughters, of course her parents wanted a boy. She and her mother never seemed to bond, and Kendall's path to womanhood was a rocky one. I asked her once how she had done it alone, saying, "You must have had a good father, or sister, or somebody there for you."

She answered, "I had a good Kendall." She paused, swallowed, and continued, "My mother was never around. I was five years old when I wanted her to fire my nurse and take care of me herself. So I figured out that my mother had a problem about dirt. I knew we had a dust closet that the nurse would lock me into if I was naughty, as when I refused to eat my cereal. (My 'crimes' usually were about not eating because I was very skinny.) I also knew my mother would be furious if she found out about the punishment, and I was sure she would fire the nurse for putting me there. So one day while my mother was out I made up a plan. On her return, as soon as the front door slammed shut I began to sob and yell loudly. Mother asked what the matter was and I told her the nurse had locked me in the dust closet. My mother stomped to the closet door and opened it in a rage. 'How could you lock a child in the dust closet with all those germs?' she yelled, dramatically raising her nose, shoulder, and hand. I was elated, fully expecting that now the nurse would have to leave and my mother would take care of me herself. It was hard not to smile. I am out of the closet, can dry my eyes, and am so happy that I am going to have my mother at last!"

And then Kendall declared like a bewildered child, "She goes to the telephone immediately and calls the agency. 'I am firing the nurse you sent me,' she asserts, 'because she had the nerve to lock my five year old daughter in the dust closet. I want you to find someone for me right away who will know how to take care of a child properly!'

"Well, my world disintegrated," Kendall continued. "I

146

can feel it now. I knew for certain that I would never, ever have my mother! I was absolutely smashed, shattered. At that moment I gave up on her forever. I knew I'd never have her and would never turn to her again.

"A few weeks later I became sick with scarlet fever. (I'm sure there is a connection.) The new nurse was there taking care of me. I thought maybe my mother would come in to see me. What she did was open the door and stand there-she had a mask on-and she didn't even come inside. She wouldn't come in – she said – because it was quarantined. But I remember thinking to myself, the new nurse is here and sitting next to me and she doesn't even have a mask on. So it was a double hurt. It absolutely formed my life. I hardly talked at all after that. I became an autistic child. I remember when I was still with the new nurse in the room she said to my mother at the door, 'She doesn't talk much, does she, madam?'

"I remember something else. The nurse said to me, 'You cut out paper dolls very well'. I guess I remember that because she gave me a compliment. My mother never did. She never played with me or liked anything I did."

Such was Kendall's portentous introduction to the world. Improbably, she climbed the heights from there, but her swan song was equally catastrophic.

Disaster conceals its beginnings well, and folds them into the work of the day. In New York, where we had seen each other perhaps twice a week, Kendall seemed fine. But when she moved to Key West a month after I got there, her life took on a different ambiance. My son Zane had given Kendall a book he wrote called *The Manic and Depressive Survival Guide*. Although she valued it deeply and was honored that he had made her a present of it, she couldn't remember what she had done with it. We frantically walked back down Duval Street until we entered the little boutique where she had left it. I didn't mind that time at all. But it soon became evident that we could never go to a restaurant or a movie that Kendall didn't forget something; a jacket, a book, her purse. It was a rare trip when she didn't lose a suitcase, a bag, or a book. We would retrace our steps and look for the article. Although Kendall often succeeded in

147

finding it, the constant trek to retrieve lost articles became more and more annoying.

Writing this makes me so sad I'll have to stop for a while...

April 3

Kendall was studying to pass the Florida licensing exam for psychologists, and I tried to help her. She was impossible, mislaying papers, finding herself hopelessly lost in a profusion of incomprehensible directions, not remembering how to fill out questionnaires even when they were explained to her over and over again. A psychologist friend who was also trying to help her wrote on one form, "You dummy!" Things got so bad that the secretarial service threw up their hands and returned her work unfinished. Kendall finally gave up the task and returned her application to the Florida Licensing Board. A few months later she was diagnosed with senile dementia. Perhaps it was Alzheimer's, I really don't know.

But at that time I didn't realize that my friend was ill. I considered her depressed, and found myself increasingly irritable in her presence. I didn't enjoy being with her anymore. She wasn't fun the way she used to be. Sometimes I even lashed out at her for what seemed like stupidity. When I recall it, my cheeks burn. Once, to my shame, I choose to go out alone with another friend, when Kendall had expressed a wish to accompany us. How I wish I had realized sooner what was going on! I guess maybe denial was at work there after all. I rationalize that Kendall's inability to function left her depressed, and it is difficult to tell how much of a personality change is depression and how much physical deterioration. Her personality changed like a chameleon; she became a real curmudgeon and wasn't even likeable. Confidences made to her received stereotyped answers. After a while, I didn't bother to explain. She even lost her famous sense of humor. I missed her quips like, "I've had the best of life and it ain't so hot!" I remember with a twinge how often we had giggled together like a pair of kindergartners.

Our friendship of almost twenty years was going

148

down the drain, along with Kendall's health. She grew worse and worse, until one day she accused me of changing the message on her answering machine. A chill ran down my windpipe as Kendall demanded to know, "Why did you put your voice on my machine?" Soon her daughter decided it was dangerous for Kendall to live alone, and insisted on moving her to an apartment in a retirement village near the family home in California. Neither the move nor various doctors helped, and Kendall rapidly deteriorated even further. I tried not to think about it. Sometimes feelings are too huge for the heart to hold.

A few months after Kendall left, I received the following pieces in the mail:

Drowning in Air

My days are filled with anomalies. How can I understand them? Where am I? A long time ago I understood readily. Today I am forced to look, look again, and I don't know where I am. Many months ago when I had a stroke my speech began to play tricks on me. Now I live in a twilight zone. For example I found a letter to be mailed. I finally found an envelope. Oh dear, I got the wrong one. I went back to get my check to put in the envelope but couldn't figure out where the address was. Was it for Virginia or Margery? I didn't know. I went to put on the address and made a mistake in spelling. Then I sealed the letter but found it was the wrong flap. It should have been opened in the top flap of the letter, not the down one. So I struggled with that. At other times I am lucid and remember how I used to be. I have a good friend who is with me a lot and helps me to straighten out the tangle. My daughter and my friend help me to remain sane, but there are many lapses.

When this first happened I tried to cover it up but soon I realized that was foolish. I had to face it. One of the first things we did was to go to an acupuncturist. The next step was to find a good physician. I am going to see him in a few weeks. This feels good because I hope that someone can help me with my speech and my memory.

Today I am very lucid. I went down to Long's drug store to get some medicine but I got in a tizzy because I couldn't find exactly what I wanted. I get furious when I can't find the particular pills I have always used. I grumble that I can't get what I want since it has been discontinued. Ugh! When nothing interferes with me I am fine. When I can't find the words I need I go bananas.

I went to see the movie *The River Runs Through It* or something like that. I liked the story a lot but many times I didn't catch some of the repartee, and then it feels like I'm in another land where I don't know the language. I want to ask but it's really not possible to keep interrupting the movie.

Reading remains a consolation. It doesn't play tricks on me and I can always look back if I don't understand something. It is a real joy, one of the few things I still find comforting, particularly if it is a good story.

Dawnings and Heartaches

I went crazy and got so tangled up with all the wrong information that I had to call my neighbor. She immediately said she would take care of it. I had already been on the phone with about ten different people and was totally unnerved.

I was working with my bookkeeper when we had an argument. She believed she was absolutely right and I was wrong. I was furious and would not give in. What was worse, she snapped at me, What you need is a nurse! My daughter must have gotten wind of the altercation and happened to appear at that moment. She solved the problem but I was crying and felt awful.

Agonizing

Well, I started out to wash the clothes today. I found, however, that I put the dirty wet wash in the dryer. Having discovered that, I went to get some tea and crackers. Instead I forgot about it and began looking for my checks and date book. Of course neither one could be found. You cannot imagine how much difficulty I have in getting through my simple day to day life. I retype many words over and over; I seem never to be able to keep track of anything. The simplest mistake seems to turn me upside down and I dwell on things all the time. Where is? Which is? Are the words or sentences spelled right? Am I making any sense of the sequence of words? It is agonizing.

April 25

Kendall soon began dropping mysterious remarks such as, "The world won't have Kendall to kick around much longer!" To my everlasting pain, I managed to tell myself that it was just Kendall's warped sense of humor returning, her take off on Nixon's infamous words to the press. She'd been saying for years she would kill herself when she got old. How was I to know that this time she meant it?

"Slay us," Ovid said, "nature or God, if you choose or if you must, but slay us in the light[109]." The death of Kendall's spirit before her body passed away was an outrage committed by nature on her dignity that she refused to tolerate.

April 30

Kendall's last letter to me said:

"I believe that for me there are few good ways to go. I would have to suffer living a slow and worrisome death. Many people are stoic, others are troublesome, but some, like myself, want to get it over with as soon as possible. One fantasy I have had for a long time. I want to go hang gliding. That seemed like such fun and such an outrageous thing to do and I do like being outrageous. I wouldn't like to smash myself on the ground, however, but I would go down over the ocean and feel safe lying quietly still in the water with nothing to fear. That may feel crazy to others but for me it would be a kind thing to do.

"It was only last night that I was talking to myself about my "condition," whatever that is. I am perpetually frightened that I will say the wrong thing, or that I do not know what the fear is all about. If I were ill or deteriorating I would certainly find a way to allow myself to let down slowly and go quietly in my sleep. My loved ones could visit. I could say whatever they wanted to hear and then I could let go and be done with it."

But still I didn't comprehend. When I reread the

letter now it is inconceivable that I didn't hear what Kendall was saying. The thought of Kendall killing herself was too appalling to allow into my consciousness, the final act of an excruciating illness. Now I wish, oh how I wish, I had been a larger human being who could have faced the truth about my friend. Then I would have flown out to California to see her before she died. Oh Kendall, I'm so sorry. Forgive me, my dear friend, won't you?

May 1

When I first met Kendall, she was celebrating her sixtieth birthday. She was only fifty-nine. She said she was observing her sixtieth birthday a year early because she wanted to get it over with. Outrageous was the word for Kendall. Her mother called her that, and she was right.

She was plagued by age spots, and tried hard to get rid of them, covering them with lemon juice and whatever medication she could find. One day she and I were walking along under the bright Key West sun. Kendall had just bought some underpants and was carrying them home. She took out a pair and wrapped it around her head. I walked a few steps behind Kendall, so nobody would think we were together.

To minimize the heat in her home, Kendall often walked around wearing only a wet tee-shirt. When she bent over to pick up the phone, her derriere (and worse) was exposed. If an unexpected guest arrived, that was just too bad.

I remember the time I was with Kendall after an old relative died. She said, "Good! I'm delighted. He is finally out of his misery." She believed that when life deteriorates to the point where pain is greater than pleasure, it is time to go. Her death was consistent with her philosophy of life.

Money didn't exist for Kendall the way it does for most people. It was as if she lacked a gene most people have. Money was there to be spent for herself and the people she cared about. Similarly, her considerable energy, which lasted to the day she died.

When my son Zane was sick with an appalling spell of mania, I felt I couldn't have gotten through it without her

152

support and sympathy. Nobody could be with you like Kendall. I think that was the secret of her magnetism, that when she was with you she was there heart and soul, putting aside all other matters. She made you feel you were the only person on earth who mattered. And for that moment, you really were. When she went to the hospital with me to visit Zane, she had previously made a lunch date with her lover, Carl. When he protested, she said simply, "That's what I have to do." It still moves me to tears to think about it.

When Zane was about to get married in the small out of the way town of Manahawken, New Jersey, my sister called and said her car had broken down and she and her family wouldn't be able to make the wedding. Kendall got on the phone and said, "Take a taxi from Philadelphia to here immediately. I will pay for it." It cost her two hundred dollars and fifty dollars, and she never said another word about it.

She gave me the most wonderful birthday present I ever received. Before any of my books were printed, I was desperate for a publication. Unbeknownst to me, Kendall had gathered together all my journal articles and poetry and had them privately printed. She nonchalantly handed me a copy of "Aspects of Psychoanalysis," casually commenting, "Happy birthday!" But her voice cracked as she said it. I know I will never again have a friend like Kendall.

Once I made the mistake of admiring her library ladder. At my next birthday, a beautiful antique ladder arrived at my home. It cost fifteen hundred dollars. I said, "Kendall, why did you spend so much money?" She answered flippantly, "Oh, it made more sense than to go all over town looking for a ladder."

Henry Johnson, Kendall, and several other therapists shared a vacation home on Three Mile Island, North Carolina for a while. The owners had a policy of not giving gifts to each other that cost over three dollars. Henry wanted a superb coffee table art book by Georgia O'Keefe, and Kendall was upset that her other housemates wouldn't allow her to buy it for him. After she died, I had to resist getting the book for Henry, as a gift from our mutual friend.

Unlike the early days of our friendship, when nothing

was too intimate for us to discuss, Kendall and I didn't talk often after she left town. I suppose it was too painful to face the separation and deterioration of our relationship. It was easier just to retain fond memories.

One morning I felt a strange pull to phone Kendall. There was no reason I knew of, I just felt I had to call. I picked up the phone, asked myself, "Why bother?" and walked away. Two minutes later I was back at the phone dialing.

"How are you, Kendall?" Silence. Then in a shaking voice, "Is everything all right?"

"Well...no."

"What do you mean? What's wrong?" My heart plummeted to my stomach. I already knew what was wrong.

"You know I've always told you that when life is no longer worth living, I want to die. I said I would kill myself when I got to be eighty. Well, I am seventy-eight and a half now, and that is enough...

I began to cry.

"I said to my daughter you were the only person I couldn't tell about it. She said she would take care of it. But I guess somehow you knew."

I couldn't think of what to say. If I said much or went out to visit Kendall, I knew I would plead with her not to kill herself. In my head I believe people have the right to die if they want to.

Kendall broke the silence. "We have a doctor out here who's going to help. I can't tell you much about it-I want to protect him. It's going to be in a few days. My children will be around me when I take the pills. My daughter will let you know."

Long silence. "I love you, Kendall."

She said, "I know." I couldn't bear to remember the rest of the conversation. When I tried my legs turned to custard pudding and I nearly passed out. My psyche is too weak to tolerate any large dose of greatness.

"Oh Kendall," I sobbed after we had hung up. "How could you do this? You love flowers so much. Won't you miss the blossoms in the springtime? How can you bear to leave the sparkle in your grandchildren's eyes? Don't you want to

154

see what becomes of them when they grow up? Suppose one wins a Nobel prize and you never know about it? Wouldn't you be sorry then? How awful your childhood must have been, for you to take so little joy in living now! And yet, you didn't always feel so pessimistic. Your article in *Voices* tells a different story."

May 12

Apparently waiting to hear that Kendall was dead was too much for me.

I dreamed that I was reading a newspaper story about two birds, which were the color of the dazzling sapphire blue vase Kendall had sent me for my last birthday. I was annoyed because the last column of the article was missing.

The bluebirds of happiness. When I woke up I thought, what lovely birds we were together! But the chips are not all down yet; the last column of the story is missing. Kendall may yet change her mind.

But she didn't. The news of her death came from her son with a dull impact that told me what I didn't want to know. I retired to my bedroom for days, where I lay curled up in my bed. I never stopped ruminating, Should I have pleaded with Kendall not to kill herself? Would it have done any good? Probably not. Was there anything I could have said or done to make her change her mind? I can't think of what it could be. We truly loved each other. But we no longer were the same people, and our relationship changed along with us. It's sad it had to do that.

In the dark of night I'm sure it's all my fault, that if I hadn't let our friendship collapse, she would still be alive, that I will never stop feeling guilty as long as I live. But then I tell myself that people grow in different ways, and there was nothing I or anyone else could do about it. The truth is this; she simply didn't want to live anymore. There was nothing I could do or say that could have made any difference.

May 13

Kendall never did anything the way anybody else did.

She spent her last days planning her own memorial. Her son said that her spirits perked up and it was the first time in a long while she seemed to be happy. The service was held at the lovely Water Club on FDR Drive in New York City where most of her friends and family lived, and Kendall herself made up the program and list of people to be invited. They included her children, grandchildren, sister, nieces, and close friends. The ceremony, she instructed, was not to be sad, but a celebration of her life and humor. Those who wished could tell Kendall stories. She directed that a slew of balloons be released at the end of the memorial. The celebrants were to write messages for her on them.

Kendall's daughter Myrna was the first to speak. She said that once when she was little, she woke up in the middle of the night scared that she would die. She ran to her mother, sat on her lap and said, "I'm just a small drop in the bucket of the universe." Her mother nodded yes.

"She taught me early about reality," Myrna said.

Then she told of asking her mother as a teenager if it was okay if she had sex.

"No," Kendall answered. Later she told Myrna, "It was going to be no as long as you had to ask!"

Kendall stories abounded, many dealing with her complete lack of modesty. She had a lovely figure and thought nothing of walking around nude in front of both men and women, singly or in groups. There was a Jacuzzi in her elegant Central Park West apartment, and she was able to convince many respectable people to bathe together naked. One therapy group held all their meetings there, sans clothing, of course. A friend spoke of how he had been married for forty years, and the only nude pictures he ever saw of his wife were those taken by Kendall in her hot tub.

A beefy, gray haired cousin told of the time he came to visit Kendall, and she said "Let's go take a Jacuzzi."

"But Kendall, we're cousins!" he protested.

"I don't give a damn, do you?" she answered. He thought, "Hmmmm, she has a beautiful figure! Why not?" When he left, she invited him to return any time he was in the city.

I smiled at the memory of Kendall's immodesty, but

didn't mention that she was the only person I knew who owned a bathroom without a door. While the Jacuzzi was being built, the workmen discovered there wasn't enough space for a door if the Jacuzzi was to be as large as Kendall wanted.

"Well, which d'ya want, the big Jacuzzi or the door?" a worker asked.

"The big Jacuzzi, of course," Kendall answered. And proceeded to go about her business, seldom checking on who if anyone was in the vicinity. Fortunately, she had a smaller bathroom for the use of more modest guests.

The memorial proceeded like a standup comedy. Another friend told how she had talked Kendall into taking a walk with her, despite her distaste for exercise. About ten minutes into the walk she asked, "Is this eternal?" The woman also spoke of going on vacation with Kendall, who asked after a few days, "When is this heavenly vacation going to end?"

A former patient of Kendall's disclosed an incident that happened in her therapy. The woman wanted to get a divorce, but was unable to leave her husband. Her paralysis took the form of an inability to pack up her books. Week after week dragged by, and still the books remained in her living room.

Finally, Kendall said, "Have you packed up your books yet?"

"No," the woman answered.

"I've been giving your situation a lot of thought," Kendall said, "and I decided it is my fault. It is my counter transference. Your conflict reminds me too much of my own divorce. So I have decided to refund your money."

"She's the only therapist I ever heard of who refunded a patient's money," the ex-patient said to the roaring crowd.

Richard, Kendall's son-in-law, said that the entertainment committee director in the retirement home where she lived asked her to help cut up birthday and Christmas cards to fill a basket with postcards for Bingo prizes. She didn't really want to do it and said she would think about it.

157

When Richard saw her the next day, he said, "What did you decide to do about the post cards?"

She answered, "I told him I'd like to help him, but I'm very unreliable."

Her tall, shapely granddaughter Serena laughingly said that when she was a bashful young teenager, her grandmother took her to buy her first bra. She loudly called to a floorwalker in the lingerie department in a voice that echoed all over Bloomingdale's, "Where are the training bras sold?"

Serena then told of what it was like to go to the movies with Kendall. "She didn't believe in waiting and would barge into the front of the line to buy her tickets. She was always chilly, and went to the theatre armed with a sweater, a blanket, and long johns, which she was not above putting on in her seat if she felt cold. If she was still uncomfortable, she would stomp out to the manager and demand that he turn down the air conditioning. If he refused, she would grope around the walls until she found the temperature control, and regulate it herself."

Serena said that although she was embarrassed then, her grandmother's straight-forward manner is now a model for her own behavior. "When I was coming here on the airplane, I had to go to the bathroom, but all the economy restrooms were filled," she said. "I was tempted to go into the empty first class bathroom, but thought it was forbidden. Then I heard my grandmother's voice say, 'You can pee in first class!' So I did."

My daughter Janet broke the festive air of the memorial. "I was told that this was to be a party in Kendall's honor," she said, "planned by Kendall herself. It was to be filled with laughter and happy memories. But I decided to pull a Kendall Kane and say what is on my mind.

"I remember going to the theater with Kendall, my mother, and Carl, her handsome boyfriend. I thought, hmmmm, this lady knows how to live! She struck me as a tall, statuesque woman who was no great beauty yet had a certain attractiveness about her. Her hair was salt and pepper, thick with a beautiful wave to it. My mother and I wondered how she styled it to give it that thick, lustrous

158

look. She told us 'mousse' so we tried it, but it never worked for us. She was dressed that night in her typical elegant yet ethnic fashion, a simple black leotard and a flowing Indian style skirt. She frequently wore interesting jewelry, necklaces in particular, little sculptures in silver circling her neck.

"We needed a cab after the show. Despite the fact that she had a bad cold, she rushed out into the street in her flowing black cape to frantically hail a taxi. Carl yelled as she ran after the taxi, 'There goes the sick woman!'

"Kendall had 'chutzpah!'" Janet continued. "If she was sitting in the first row center of a theater and decided in the middle of the act that she didn't like the play, she would get up and leave. If the actors were disturbed, she felt that was not her problem.

"Kendall was a professor emeritus at City College, a prolific writer, a therapist who delved into alternate types of therapy such as attending Gestalt weekend retreats. She touched many lives, as they read her books, attended her classes, or became patients in her practice.

"In a recent project, she videotaped famous living analysts at the end of their careers. I watched some of the tapes and thought they were brilliant. They are now in the archives of a great university, held in custody for posterity.

"Kendall was a Jewish mother, especially when it came to her son Dick. She was always looking for the perfect match for him, even to sorting through the letters he received from an ad placed the personal columns in the *New York Review of Books*. Naturally, she was the one who had placed the ad. Since Dick said he wanted to marry a woman with children, the ad began, 'Too old to start from scratch!'

"Kendall was also a JAP, the code word for Jewish American Princess. The Mamaroneck housewife in her frequently surfaced. She hosted my bridal shower with great elegance and finesse, and prepared a gracious luncheon served on the finest china and silver. Kendall baked the cake herself, a white chocolate mousse adorned with flowers. She had a lovely garden of roses on the patio outside her bedroom. Her apartment was always filled with plants and flowers. Her home looked like a country estate in the middle of Manhattan.

"Kendall hated to eat in restaurants," Janet said with a smile. "I frequently accompanied my mother to Kendall's apartment for dinner, where she would stand in her small kitchen and whip up a gourmet meal. I found out later she had taken a course in Cordon Bleu cooking in Paris. She enjoyed cooking for my mother because she loved to cook and also because my mother was so appreciative. Kendall would cook special low-fat dinners, adding a touch of forbidden foods and joking with me, a nutritionist, about how it wouldn't really hurt. She would sneak my mother some high-fat desert with a smile, knowing I wouldn't approve but reveling in my mother's childish pleasure.

"In restaurants, Kendall would always offer to pay the bill. If I mentioned I liked something, it would not be unlike her to give it to me. Once she accompanied my family on a barge trip to Southern France. Kendall was practically a member of the family, and not at all out of place. We were in a small French village when we stumbled upon a children's clothing store. My daughter Rachel was then ten months old. I saw an adorable two piece outfit I wanted to buy but it was too expensive. Kendall bought it for Rachel." Janet's voice broke as she added, "I will always treasure the memory."

"Kendall was generous with much more than money. She gave of herself to others in need. When my mother was hit by a car, it was Kendall who had me stay at her house, had me take a Jacuzzi, and even found my mother the best doctor in New York. As I look back on the many faces of Kendall Kane, I feel the loss of a surrogate mother, grandmother, and comforting friend. Kendall's outstretched arms, touching hand made me feel better in times of need. Her words were soothing, her touch gentle.

"And so, I remember Kendall Kane. I will always miss her."

I was the last speaker of the memorial. My heart was full of sorrow, and despite Kendall's request, I knew I couldn't pull off any jokes about the death of my dear friend.

"Kendall didn't want this to be a sad occasion," I began. "But perhaps she will forgive me if I quote Alfred Lord Tennyson[110] on how I feel about her leaving us:
Break, Break, Break

Break, break, break
    On thy cold gray stones, O Sea!
And I would that my tongue could utter
    The thoughts that arise in me.

Like Ted Kennedy giving the eulogy for his brother Bobby at Saint Patrick's Cathedral, my voice splintered, and I could barely finish the lines, "I would that my tongue could utter/The thoughts that arise in me." But I sucked in my breath and completed the poem:

O well for the fisherman's boy,
    That he shouts with his sister at play!
O well for the sailor lad,
    That he sings in his boat on the bay!

And the stately ships go on
    To their haven under the hill;
But O for the touch of a vanish'd hand,
    And the sound of a voice that is still!

Break, break, break
    At the foot of thy crags, O Sea!
But the tender grace of a day that is dead
    Will never come back to me.

Then I read Kendall's Drowning in Air, which she had forwarded shortly before her death.

As we left the Water Club, my children and I stood watching the balloons glide up, up, up, until they were consumed by the hazy mist. One carried Zane's message, "See you again, but hopefully not too soon." In the distance a foghorn moaned into the night. Reluctant to say their final good-byes, a few mourners lingered on inside the club. A guest's shrill piercing laugh drifted out over the river. It was the saddest sound I ever heard.

May 29
A few weeks after the memorial I had another dream.
I was standing on top of a steep hill of ice. I looked

161

down and there was a sheer drop, like an abyss. There was only a narrow path you could streak down on a sled. I didn't know how I could do it. I told a little boy who looked like my son Jonny that I was terrified to go down the hill, but would anyway.

Beside the hilltop, I stumbled into a warm booklined building, paneled in brown wood. On one of the top floors, I passed a large ward filled with old and crippled patients. I looked inside and then kept on walking. Wrought iron stairs led to the ground floor. I walked down slowly, and was overcome with a feeling of pleasure. The 'down hill trip' turned out to be a joy and not frightening at all.

The next day I sat with bowed head and streaming eyes, seeped in sorrow at the loss of my dearest friend. My mind wandered over the many good times we had shared, how much we laughed and cried together, Kendall's generosity, how funny she was, how available when needed, the fact that there was nothing in the world I couldn't tell Kendall and have it understood, and how much I had learned from her. Once more I relived Kendall's ghastly decline, and again chastised myself for not recognizing the severity of her illness.

"How could I, how could I not have known?" I castigated myself. "I knew you so well, Kendall. I am a psychologist. I can't believe I refused to see." I scrutinized once more the events of that awful year to try to find where, if anywhere, I could have interceded to save Kendall's life. But I found no occasion where an intervention could have made the fateful difference. "All meetings end in departures. All commitments are destined to end," say the Buddhist monks. Kendall knew she was loved. Neither my devotion nor that of her children and grandchildren was enough to keep her alive. The truth was that Kendall had enough of life. She wanted only to die. "The long day's task is done./ And we must sleep[111]."

Readers may find it strange in a book about death that I have not gone deeply into the question of euthanasia. I haven't done so because I, who have an opinion about practically everything, have nothing conclusive to say about suicide. True, Kendall's lethal act caused a great deal of pain.

But then I'm sure she carefully weighed the cost of staying alive versus the distress her death would cause others. Who was in a better position than Kendall to know how the scales balanced? I can only contend that while I wish she had desisted, her action is understandable. There is no final answer that holds true for all people who want to take their lives. In my opinion, suicide is not a moral issue, but rather a question of what is best for the individual and those who love him or her. I don't believe I (or anyone else) have the right to judge. Kendall did what she had to do. Let her rest in peace.

What in Kendall could have allowed her to accept that she had enough of life? Life is so rich - so crammed with joy and sorrow, love and hate, fascination, hope, learning, creativity, and simple pleasures like the unexpected phone call or letter in the mail, chocolate ice cream on a hot night, the thank you for a long forgotten word, the smell of the surf, the sight of the shimmering sea beneath the sunset in Key West - that I can't understand choosing to sleep under the sod. As King Lear said to his dead daughter, I ask you, Kendall, "Why should a dog, a horse, a rat, have life, /And thou no breath at all[112]?"

Then Ed Griffin, an ex-priest and dear writer friend told me of someone who found an answer to my question, at least for himself. Cardinal Joseph Bernadin, the great archbishop of Chicago, said shortly before his death on November 15, 1996[113]:

"There's something that I've become aware of: as you enter into the dying process, that process prepares you for death as you slow down. For example, I have no great desire to accomplish a lot of things before I go. I'm writing a few reflections; if I finish I finish; if I don't finish I don't finish. My legacy is what I have accomplished or have not accomplished in the last four and a half decades....And that gives you a certain amount of peace, so that leads me to say: Yes. I'm ready now. It's not that there's not a certain sadness to it. That, too, is part of the human condition. But I'm totally reconciled to the fact that before too long, I'm going to go, and I think I will be ready for it."

It is interesting that Cardinal Bernadin's wisdom was

preceded in a sonnet by Edna St. Vincent Millay[114], who sensed on an instinctual level the revelation that came to the Cardinal in his illness:

I dread no more the first white in my hair,
Or even age itself, the easy shoe,
The cane, the wrinkled hands, the special chair;
Time, doing this to me, may alter too
My anguish, into something I can bear.

It may be that I am so angry at the thought of dying because I am not ready yet. Perhaps Freud was wrong in saying that no person can accept his own mortality. Perhaps when he said that, he wasn't ready either. In his old age, when he had inoperable cancer, he too gave up his wish to live and killed himself. Perhaps Dylan Thomas, who wrote "Do not go gentle into that good night," was not ready to go yet, either. And perhaps Cardinal Bernadin could go gentle into that good night because he was ready. Perhaps Kendall could leave this life because she, too, was ready to go. And perhaps like Cardinal Bernadin, when my time comes the dying process will prepare me for death.

Suddenly the memory of what Kendall had said at the end of our last phone call returned like a clap of thunder. I heard her husky, resonant voice as clearly as if she were in the room. Speaking in her droll, half-serious manner, she said:

"Think of me when you go over a bridge, and a cool breeze flutters against your forehead. Think of me when the warm sun caresses your cheek, or when a phrase of music gladdens your heart. Think of me when the poincianas bloom, and know they have blossomed for us both. Think of me between the pitter-patter of the raindrops. And if you need to talk with me, put your fingers on your pulse and listen for my voice. And know I am always there."

I remembered her words between the teardrops. Then I placed my fingers on my pulse and listened until I felt the strength of her aura around me. It was unmistakably Kendall, of that I had no doubt. I said, "I can't write anymore, Kendall. If you were alive we would have talked about it and you would have helped me get over it. Can you

164

help me now?"

Kendall answered, "Enough of this stalling, Alma! Get to work. You have a lot to say. You don't need any help."

Swallowing the knob in my throat, I said, "Thank you, my friend. I knew you would come through for me!" Then I threw back my head, straightened my back, and sat down to begin my new book, *Magnificent Monster: the Story of Margaret Mahler.*

Finale

I cannot leave this book without passing along to you, dear reader, the enormous insights that have come about from writing these memoirs, as I faced the intense emotions that arose when I confronted once again the beloved figures of the past. Somehow, the writing of an autobiography creates an atmosphere for the welling up of memories. And sometimes, as Proust said, "The memories that emerge from oblivion are more beautiful than the experiences themselves[115]." In reviewing my life and the lives of my friends, I have been able to distill the memories of years of friendship to discover the unique value each relationship had and has for me. I always loved these women, but writing their memoirs has enabled me to understand far better the place each held in my life and development.

My late husband's character (which requires a book of its own to do it justice) deserves credit for the beginning of this odyssey. My quest for insight into the fear of death began with the dream in which Rudy shrewdly if inelegantly says that all my efforts to extend my life are nothing but "horse piss." The directness of his observation epitomized his blunt manner, his emotional honesty, and his awareness that there is nothing one can do to escape the painful exigencies of life. Just as I learned from his candor in other areas of our lives, I was able to embrace "his" interpretation of my dream, and to begin the long voyage leading to the acceptance of my own mortality.

What did I learn from the death of Shirley Syms? Mostly I found that we cannot always control our destinies. Just as my conception, arrival into this world, choice of parents, siblings, time and country of birth, intelligence, appearance, and the formation of much of my character had nothing to do with my own wishes, my relationship with Shirley taught me that there is nothing we can do about the deaths of people we care about but to endure them in the best ways we can find. Similarly, I learned to live with the fact that some people I love may not return my feelings, and that it is not worth dying over. Perhaps most significantly, I learned from Shirley Syms that the moment of my own death cannot be under my control. To have it my way would be far too costly.

And Joan's death, what did I learn from that? Perhaps the most important psychological insight I gained in over forty years of psychoanalytic study. My grief for Joan brought me in touch with my own death wishes and the wish to join her, and demanded that I question whether, despite my happy, fulfilled life, I really wished to die. Edgar Allen Poe in *The Raven*[116] sought death to bring him "surcease of sorrow, of memories of Lenore." I, too, am seeking relief from the pain of losing those dear to me, and from much else in life I find unbearable. In death no regrets will plague me, no unrequited needs, no inner pain, no sorrow, no longing, no destruction, no loss. As in my first Shirley Syms dream, I could languidly repose among the trees and flowers forever, even if I were unaware of them. Yes, death will bring its "surcease of sorrow." But not now, not soon, in fact not ever, if I have any say in the matter! I'd much rather live with the anguish, so that I can gently touch my grandchildren, look into the eyes of my children with love, relish the time left with remaining friends, glory in the sunset over the gulf stream in Key West, and finish all the books I have left in me to write.

Thus the main lesson for me of Joan's death was that

I had to experience all the strength of my wish to die, before I could learn that strong as the pull toward death is, the life urge in me is even more powerful. For the more conscious in us the wish to die, the less strong is the tug towards death, and the longer we are likely to stay alive.

Anna Schwartz was my first close friend. Through her, I learned the joy of intimacy, of companionship, of having a playmate, a confident, an advisor. The values I learned from Anna have remained guideposts in my life. Because of Anna's unique sense of style, I learned from her how to dress, the use of color and symplicity of line, principles I still use today. Anna made her life her art, and demonstrated that the usual exigencies of home and family can be as satisfying as anything else in life. Since my parents were immigrants and unfamiliar with the ways of America, Anna also became my social guide. She taught me how to behave appropriately on social occasions, how to date, to issue invitations, to give a party, which fork to use at a formal dinner. Without her, my passage through the convolutions of growing up would have been far more difficult.

Transitions are painful without a model. Now that I am growing old, I miss Anna more than ever. But sometimes when I feel lost and baffled by the complexities of aging, I talk to Anna. Her wisdom, common sense, and intuitive knowledge are always there to guide me.

And what about my beloved Jill? What I learned from her death is so intertwined with what she taught me in life that the two cannot be separated. When I met Jill, I was a love starved adolescent and she an "older woman." I was not yet ready to marry, although I already was in love with Rudy and knew I wanted to have his children. I also loved many women but shied away from giving or receiving affection from any of them. Why was I so foolish? First of all, my family members were not touchers, and I had never learned to physically express my feelings. But perhaps more important, I was afraid of my need for women and was terrified of becoming a homosexual (whatever that meant to me at the time) and losing my dream of having a loving husband and children. What I learned from Jill's tender touch was that people can be caring and affectionate with each other without necessarily being gay. As a wise patient discovered to her (and my) delight many years later, "Everyone had both a father and a mother. Why wouldn't we love both sexes?"

When I felt Jill's gentle fingers on my head after she died, I learned that the healing power of a loving touch endures long after the toucher has departed. I understand what Elizabeth Barrett Browning[117] felt about Robert Browning when she wrote, "I shall but love thee better after death."

Kendall knew me better than anyone else did in the whole world and loved me anyway. Her unpolluted feeling for me was the closest I've ever come to knowing unconditional love.

Kendall's article in *Voices*[118] reflects better than I could the essence of Kendall Kane. Somehow, somewhere, in the mysterious labyrinth of character development, she learned to accept her own shortcomings. And since she could tolerate her own flaws, she was also able to accept those of people she loved. I come from a family of critical women, and self-criticism was a part of my daily routine. Kendall changed all that. I never liked myself so much as when I understood that Kendall accepted me for my weaknesses as much as my strengths.

"Your shortcomings make you more human," she said. "Otherwise you'd be impossible. As you almost are," she added under her breath. She left me a superb legacy: She taught me to like myself.

I try to emulate Kendall's policy of honesty at all costs, although I have never learned to implement it as well as she did. But because of her tutelage, I've become a more honest mother, friend, and writer. If you find this an honest book, reader, give some of the credit to Kendall Kane.

On reading over these last few pages, I've come to a conclusion I long suspected but never really celebrated. This book is that long overdue celebration. How lucky I am to have been blessed with such wonderful, wise, loving, generous friends! Whether they are alive or dead, I carry them around inside of me, and thus I can never lose them.

In order to try to help other people who wish above all to stay alive, I would like to stress that the review of my life and the lives of my friends have led to a renewed belief in the power of the Death Instinct. I believe it is always lurking just below the surface in all of us. Life or death is only a matter of balancing the scales. If life is lived according to one's inner needs and not merely the edicts of society, the Life Instinct is strong enough to win out over the magnetic pull of the grave. If one's deepest cravings are not met, no matter how exemplary our existence, the Life Instinct recedes and the relentless undertow of the Death Instinct drags us under.

I had a neighbor once on Long Beach Island who loved her husband and wanted to be a good wife. He loved his boat, and liked to go out every day to fish. His wife, however, hated both fishing and the boat. Nevertheless, she wanted to make her husband happy. So every day she accompanied him on his fishing expeditions. And every night, yielding to her self-destructive impulses, she came home and got drunk! I'd be surprised to hear she is still alive.

Shirley Syms, devoted wife and activist for many causes, and Anna Schwartz, homemaker par excellance who lived for her family, also surrendered to the Death Instinct. Both women led exemplary existences, but the gratifications of being "good women" did not make up for their inner vacuum. And despite her magnificent attempts to sublimate her grief, I believe Joan Simonton's unhappiness over her beloved son's "deviant" sexuality was enough to drag her into the abyss from which no one ever returns. Jill and Kendall Kane were alike both in their final illnesses, and the fact that despite highly successful careers and domestic lives neither woman was able to overcome the anguish of a loveless infancy.

What is the lesson in this for you, dear reader? I suggest that if we want to stay alive we look deeply into our souls to ask what in life we want the most, and then move Heaven and Hell to obtain it. This is no idle suggestion; I believe it is a matter of life or death. I don't know what my Long Beach Island neighbor wanted in life, but I'm willing to bet it was not spending all her days fishing.

As for me, I changed careers because I felt my life depended on it. I was a wonderfully happy, successful psychoanalyst with an office off Fifth Avenue in New York City for over thirty-five years. I loved doing real analysis, in which many of the patients who came for treatment four or five times a week were able to achieve relief from their problems and create a richer, healthier life. Toward the end of my analytic practice, the insurance companies refused to pay for lengthy treatment. Patients cut down on the number of sessions, and I found myself doing more psychotherapy than psychoanalysis. As a result, my pleasure in the work greatly diminished. When one's satisfaction in work dissipates, it is time to move on, but I was not yet aware that was what I had to do.

Then I was in a car accident. A taxi traveling forty-five miles an hour in Central Park hit me and tossed me ten feet into the air. Coming down, I hit a telephone pole. I was hospitalized in intensive care, with a concussion and seven broken bones. I was not expected to live. People said it was a miracle that I survived. Whether a death wish contributed to my not seeing the taxi that hit me, I can't be sure. But I lay in a coma for days, and returned to consciousness thinking something like this, "I've had a full and happy life, with a wonderful career and a loving family. But the time of joy in my work has passed, as has my family life with the death of Rudy and the hole left in the fabric of my life when my adult children left home. It is time to move on to another phase of life." Then it came to me in a flash that the one thing I had not done was what I needed to do the most, to devote the rest of my life to writing. I understood this, but did not act on it for some time. It is not easy to give up a flourishing practice which brings one a great deal of acclaim and respect, to say nothing of money.

I asked my son Zane, who knows the value of following your heart, "Do you think I'd be crazy to give up a high-paying job for a possibly non-paying job?" He answered, "I think you'd be crazy not to."

So I began to terminate my practice, and a few years later moved to Key West to begin the writing career which

172

(so far) has led to the publication of eight books and many magazine and newspaper articles. I've never regretted my decision. My joy in writing keeps me alive.

Fine, you might say, when what you want is a change of career or locale. But what about when you are overcome with loss and grief, and what you want most is the return of a loved one? What can you do to help yourself survive?

In my opinion, it is essential for continued health to stay with one's pain until a natural cure occurs. *Pain does not kill; repression does.* If you squelch your feelings indefinitely, you will not really get well or achieve the fullness of life you are entitled to. The grief will simply go underground and rise in the future to hurt you. Many a depression is caused by unfinished grieving, and many a marriage has gone on the rocks because one of the partners has not completed the mourning process for a former mate. An outpouring of pain in one form or another is imperative. If you are experiencing life-threatening sorrow, reader, please don't delay! As I advised my recently widowed friend Harriet, speak to your family and friends about it or to anyone who will listen. Talk, talk, talk. Don't worry about imposing on them. Your life is at stake.

Perhaps you, like me, will find keeping a journal of help. It can give you insight into the relationship you had with the person who died, come to terms with your guilt, keep the person alive in your heart, and help cure your depression. Go into therapy with a grief counselor, or join a bereavement support group, in which you can all cry together about your collective losses.

Try to find sublimation for your grief. I found it in writing. Perhaps you can do the same, if not in a death diary or dream diary, in a poem, or in letters to sympathetic friends or family members. Are you an artist of sorts? Don't worry about the quality of the work, but paint, draw or sculpt images of your loved one and keep him or her with you forever. Do you sing or play an instrument? Create music that gives substance to your grief. It will help to heal your wounds.

I also recommend working for causes in the fight against what led to the death of your loved one. This will help sublimate your grief, as well as being useful to humankind. Membership in MADD (Mothers Against Drunk Driving) is highly beneficial to mothers who have lost their children to drunk drivers. AIDS Help is a wonderful source of healing for those of us who have lost dear ones to the dreadful disease. Helping to combat mental illness, cancer, kidney failure, spinal injury, SIDS, and birth defects benefits the lives of those fighting such ailments, along with your own.

Another bit of advice that helps me enjoy my remaining days. *Carpe diem*! Seize the day. Enjoy each moment as if it were your last. Who knows, perhaps it is. Today I decided to take leave of finishing this book to go see the movie *One Thousand Acres*, a modernized version of *King Lear*[119], one of my favorite plays. (I liked *King Lear* better.) The sun was shining brightly and glistening on the ocean as I drove up U.S. 1. A whiff of sea air brought the smell of salt to my nostrils, as the palm trees swayed in the gentle breezes. I thought, how wonderful that I am driving my own car on this beautiful day to go to a movie I want to see! But it's a good thing I'm enjoying it. Who knows how long I'll be able to drive, or even to see. Yes, *Carpe diem*, seize the moment. It may well be all there is. And what about the fear of death, which wise men through the ages have considered the basis of all terror? The most important aspect in fighting fear is to acknowledge it. Freud said[120], "If you want to endure life, prepare yourself for death." In acknowledging my fear, I learned to examine it, and to separate what was real from fantasy. I discovered that my apprehension at least in part was caused by my own death wishes. What I experienced as fear was really the infantile belief that wishing will make it so. When that became clear, I was able to weigh the reality of my wish to die against my desire to live, and found that the latter was far stronger. From the material in my dreams, I think it is highly likely that without this insight, I would have joined my friends.

My reading helped, especially Freud's work on the Death Instinct[121] and Ernest Becker's *The Denial of Death*[122]. I also found the words of the dying Cardinal Bernadin[123] particularly illuminating, when he wrote that as you approach death, you aren't so afraid of it. When you are ready, everything in life is easier. Thus ninety-year-old psychoanalyst Helena Deutch was able to end her autobiography with the line, "After more than fifty years of uninterrupted activity in the service of psychoanalysis I now wish for nothing more than a very long sabbatical[124]."

Some indications of immortality through my grandchildren, and hopefully, my books, also helped to soften my fears. The idea of dying is not quite as horrifying if one knows that in some manner or other one will live on.

Am I still frightened of dying? Of course. But less than I was, and more able to take it in stride. I still don't want to leave our beautiful earth, and will do everything I can to stay in good health. When it is time for me to die, I expect I will say goodbye with sadness, as well as with gratitude for a wonderful life. But as I learned from my dreams of Shirley Syms, we can't always control our lives or deaths. Que sera sera. If I have to die, so be it. Praise be to all living things!

Bibliography

1 Sacks, Oliver. <u>Island of the Colorblind.</u> New York: Alfred A. Knopf ,1997. 64.

2 Shakespeare, William. <u>Hamlet.</u> Act III, scene 1.

3 Darling, David. <u>Soul Search.</u> New York: Villard Books, a division of Random House, Inc. 43.

4 Sophocles. "Antigone." <u>Seven Famous Greek Plays.</u> New York: Random House, 1950. 199.

5 Freud, Sigmund. <u>The Standard Edition of the Complete Psychological Works of Sigmund Freud</u>. Vol. 14. London: Hogarth Press, 1975. 289-300.

6 Freud, Sigmund. On transience. <u>The Standard Edition of the Complete Psychological Works of Sigmund Freud</u>. Vol. 14. London: Hogarth Press, 1975. 306.

7 Amis, Kingsley. "Delivery Guaranteed." <u>Collected Poems.</u> Hutchinson Publishing Group Ltd. and Jonathan Clowes, Ltd.

8 Shakespeare, William. <u>Richard</u> II. Act III, scene 2. 148.

9 <u>The Holy Bible</u>. New International Version. Matthew 8:21-22; Luke 9:60.

10 Goodman, Lisl M. <u>Death and the Creative Life: Conversations with Prominent Artists and Scientists</u>. New York: Springer Publishing Company, 1981.

11 Kaplan, Alex H. "Experiencing Aging." <u>How Psychiatrists Look at Aging</u>.Vol. 2. George H. Pollack, ed. Madison: International Universities Press, 1994.42.

12 "Note left on a Doorstep."(by Lily Peter, from "The Green Linen of Summer," published in <u>A Nude Singularity</u>, by

AnnieLaura M. Jaggers, UCA Press, Conway. AR, 1993.)

13 Edna Saint Vincent Millay, <u>Collected Lyrics</u>, Lament, Harper & Row, N.Y., Evanston, & London, 1939,, p. 174.

14 Broyard, Anatole, <u>Intoxicated by my Illness</u>, Fawcett Columbine, N.Y., 1992, 20.

15 Jacques, Eliot. "Death and the Mid-Life Crisis," in <u>Death: Interpretations</u>, H.M. Ruitenbeek, Ed., N.Y.: Delta, 1969, Chapter 13, as quoted by Ernest Becker (Opus cited), 215-6.

16 Opus cited, xiii.

17 Capra, Fritjof, The Turning Point, Bantam Books, Toronto, N.Y., London, Sydney, and Aukland, p. 374.

18 Opus cited, 7.

19 Goffman, Erving. "Stigma: Notes on the Management of Spoiled Identity," 1964, Prentice-Hall, Englewood Cliffs, N.J.

20 Corinthians 15:54-55.

21 Tompkins, Calvin, "De Kooning as Melodrama," <u>The New Yorker</u>, Feb. 10, 1997, pp. 74-77

22 Ecclesiastes, 9.

23 Edna St. Vincent Millay, opus cited, p. 85.

24 Goodman, Lisl. <u>Death and the Creative Life</u>, Springer Publishing Co., U.S.A., 1981.

25 Hutchnecker, Arnold. <u>The Meaning of Death</u>, Ed: Herman Feifel, N.Y.:McGraw-Hill Books Co., Inc., 1959.

26 Atkin, Samuel and Atkin, Adam, "On Being Old," in <u>How Psychiatrists Look at Aging</u>, Ed: George H. Pollock,

International Universities Press,Madison, Ct, 1992, 14-15.

27 Terkel, Studs. <u>Coming of Age,</u> St. Martin's Griffin, N.Y., 1995, p. xv.

28 Shakespeare, William. <u>As You Like it,</u> Act 2, scene 7.

29 Ernest Becker, <u>The Denial of Death</u>, The Free Press, 1972.

30 The Merck Manual, 15th Edition. Merck and Co., Inc., Rahway, N.J., 1987, 3222-3223.

31 Koren, Edward. <u>The New Yorker</u>, July 14, 1997, , p. 53.

32 Greenspan, Robin. "Virtual Hilarity," Readers Digest, August, 1997.

33 Freud, Sigmund. <u>Beyond the Pleasure Principle</u> (1920), Standard Edition, Hogarth Press, London, 1971, pps.36-38.

34 Freud, Sigmund. <u>Beyond the Pleasure Principle</u>, Standard Edition, 39.

35 Holderlin, Friedrich. (From "Nur einen Sommer," translated by Walter Kaufmann, 1976, in "Existentialism, Religion, and Death." (in "Death and the Creative Life," by Lisl Marburg Goodman - Springer Publishing Company, USA, 1981)

36 Heynen, Jim. <u>One Hundred Over 100</u>, Fulcrum Publishing, Golden, Colorado, 1990.

37 Kotulak, Ronald. "Keeping the Brain Sharp as We Age," <u>The Saturday Evening Post</u>, Nov\Dec 1996.

38 Terkel, Studs. Opus cited. pps. xvii-xviii.

39 Cicero, in <u>The Oxford Book of Aging</u>, Ed: Thomas R. Cole & Mary G. Winkler, Oxford, NY, 1994, 49-51.

40 Kaku, Michio. <u>Hyperspace</u>, N.Y.: London, Toronto, Sydney, Aukland, 210.

41 Shakespeare, William. <u>Measure for Measure</u>, 111, i, 42.

42 Shakespeare, William. <u>The Tempest</u>, 11, i, 257.

43 I am grateful to Dr. Elizabeth Saenger for this story.

44 Jeans, Sir James. <u>The Mysterious Universe</u>, Cambridge, 1937, p. 122, f. 14.

45 Heine, Heinrich, <u>Letters on the French Stage</u>, quoted in "Opera in America", by John Dizekes.

46 Von Franz, Marie-Louise, in <u>On Dreams and Death</u>, Shambbala: Boston and London, 1986, 147.

47 Opus cited, 149.

48 Heywood, Rosalind. "Death and Psychical Research" in <u>Man's Concern with Death</u>, by Arnold Toynbee and others, Hodder and Stoughton Ltd., St. Paul's House, London EC4, England, 244.

49 Opus cited. Richard Gregory in <u>The New Scientist</u>, August 30, 1962, 244.

50 Shakespeare, William, <u>Twelfth Night</u>, V, i, 378.

51 Freedman, William. <u>Swift's Struldbruggs, progress, and the analogy of history</u>, Information Access Company, webmaster@encarta.cognito.com, 1996.

52 Sheehan, George. <u>Going the Distance</u>, N.Y.: Villard, 1996, xiii.

53 Thomas Mann, <u>The Magic Mountain</u>, Vintage Books Edition, N.Y., 1969, 292.

54 Tennyson, Alfred Lord. In Memoriam.

55 Shakespeare, William. Anthony and Cleopatra, Act 4, Scene 15.

56 Reik, Theodore, Personal Communication.

57 Chopra, Deepak. Ageless Body, Timeless Mind, Harmony Books, N.Y., p. 216.

58 Capra, Fritjof. The Turning Point, Bantam Books,Toronto, N.Y., London, Sydney, Auckland, 1088, pp. 354-355.

59 Deutsch, Helene. Confrontations with Myself, W.W. Norton, N.Y., 1973, p. 54.

60 Shakespeare, William, King Lear, 1605, Act IV, Sc. 1,1. (10-14).

61 Jung, Carl G. Memories, Dreams, Reflections, Pantheon Books, A Division of Random House, N.Y., 1963, 301.

62 M. Wohy, The New Yorker, Feb. 10, 1997, p. 80.

63 Back, Gloria Guss. Are You Still My Mother? Warner Books, NY, NY, 1985.

64 Ecclesiasticus, 38.

65 Shakespeare, William,, Julius Caesar, 111, i, 159.

66 Muhammad: From The Sayings of Muhammad, translated by Sir Abdullah al-Mamum Suhrawardy, John Murray, Ltd., 1941.

67 Shakespeare, William. King Lear.

68 Thomas Mann, The Magic Mountain.

69 Robert Burton, <u>The Anatomy of Melancholy</u>, 1621.

70 Sam Atkin. Opus cited, 14.

71 <u>New York Times Magazine</u>, 12\15\96.

72 Sun-Sentinel, Oct 19, 1996, <u>Music Review</u> by Matt Schudel.

73 The Key West Citizen, Cartoon <u>Born Loser</u>, Oct. 15, 1996.

74 Gene Fowler. <u>Good Night, Sweet Prince</u>, Viking Press, 1944, p. 1.

75 Evening Standard, 1980, in <u>The Oxford Book of Death</u>, Ed: D.J. Enright, 212.

76 Freud, E. <u>Letters of Sigmund Freud</u>, Dover, 1960, NY, 386.

77 Prodigy, <u>Study Links Alzheimer's, EMF's</u>, Dec. 18, '96.

78 Heine, Heinrich. 1856. Reprinted in <u>The Oxford Book of Death</u>, Ed: D.J. Enright, Oxford, N.Y., 1983, 331.

79 Darling, David, <u>Soul Search</u>, Villard Books, 1993, 131-133.

80 Rabelais, 1532, reprinted in <u>The Oxford Book of Death</u>, Ed: D. J. Enright, Oxford, N.Y., 1983, 330.

81 Bond, Alma H. <u>Is There Life After Analysis?</u> Wynwood Press, 1993.

82 Sarton, May. <u>At Eighty-Two</u>, N.Y. & London, W.W. Norton and Co., 251-254.

83 Gottschalk, Louis A., "On Aging,"in <u>How Psychiatrists Look at Aging (Volume 2)</u>, Ed: George H. Pollock, Madison, Ct., International Universities Press, 1994, pp.10-24.

84 Bond, Alma H. <u>Sadomasochistic Patterns in an Eighteen-Month-Old Child</u>, International Journal of Psychoanalysis, 1967, v. 48, No. 4, pp. 597-602.

85 Sophocles, <u>Woman of Trachis</u>.

86 Gray, Thomas. <u>Elegy Written in a Country Church Yard.</u>

87 Lowell, Robert. Poem found among his papers.

88 Sheehan, George. Opus cited, xiii.

89 Smith, Sally Bedell. Opus cited, p. 18.

90 Smith, Sally Bedell. Opus cited, p. 214.

91 Smith, Sally Bedell. Opus cited, p. 336-338.

92 Smith, Sally Bedell. Opus cited.

93 Rossellini, Isabella. <u>Some of Me</u>, Random House, N.Y., 1997, p. 19.

94 Rossellini, Isabella. Opus cited. p. 15.

95 Shakespeare, <u>Romeo and Juliet</u>, IV, v, 28.

96 Natchez, Gladys. The Negative Aspects of Therapeutic Change. In <u>Voices</u>. Winter,   1974-75, pp. 50-51.

97 La Rochefoucauld, Francois, Duc de. <u>Maxims</u>

98 Bond, Alma Halbert Bond. Who Killed Virginia Woolf? A Psychobiography, Human   Sciences Press, Inc., N.Y., 1989.

99 Shelley, Percy Bysshe (1818-24). Stanzas Written in Dejection, Near Naples, in <u>English   Poetry and Prose of the Romantic Movement,</u> (Ed: George Benjamin Woods), Scott,

Foresman and Co., Chicago, Atlanta, Dallas, and N.Y., 1929, pps. 654-5.

100 Kettering, Terry, The Elephant in the Room, Bereavement Publishing Inc., Colorado Springs, Colo.

101 Bond, Alma H. Profiles of Key West, poho press, Key West, 1996.

102 Forster, E.M. A Passage to India, 1924.

103 Shakespeare, William, Timon of Athens, I, ii, 147.

104 I am grateful to my friend, Dorothy Beach, for giving me this information.

105 Milton Cross' Encyclopedia of the Great composers and Their Music, Doubleday & Co., N.Y., 1962, 458.

106 Thomas, Lewis. Late Night Thoughts on Listening to Mahler's Ninth Symphony, Encarta Encyclopedia.

107 Becker, Ernest, Opus cited, 27.

108 Perls, Fritz, as quoted in Ernest Becker's The Denial of Death, Opus cited, 57.

109 Ovid, Book XVII, line 647.

110 Tennyson, Alfred Lord. "Break Break Break" in Selected Poetry. Penguin Books, N.Y., 1983, 74.

111 William Shakespeare, Anthony and Cleopatra, IV, xiv, 35.

112 Shakespeare, William. King Lear, Act 5, Scene 3.

113 NY Times Magazine, December 1, 1996.

114 Millay, Edna Saint Vincent, Collected Sonnets, Harper & Row, N.Y., Evanston, & London, 1942, cxxio, 124.

115 Proust, as quoted in <u>Confrontations with Myself</u>, by Helene Deutsch, W.W. Norton and Co., N.Y., 1973, p.13.

116 Poe, Edgar Allan. "The Raven." <u>The Viking Book of Poetry of the English-SpeakingWorld</u>, Viking Press, N.Y., 1941, p. 865.

117 Browning, Elizabeth Barrett. "How do I love thee?" <u>Viking Book of Poetry of the English</u> <u>Speaking World</u>, Viking Press, N.Y., 1941, p. 818.

118 Natchez, Gladys. Opus cited.

119 Shakespeare, William, Opus cited.

120 Freud, Sigmund. <u>Standard Edition</u>, Hogarth Press, London, V., X1V, 289-300.

121 Freud, Sigmund. Opus cited.

122 Ernest Becker, Opus cited.

123 Berndain, Cardinal Joseph. N.Y. Times. Opus cited.

124 Deutsch, Helene. <u>Confrontations with Myself</u>, W.W.Norton and Co., N.Y., 1973, p. 217.

Printed in the United States
71754LV00002B/92

9 781581 129045